CHARACTERS IN ACTION

PLAYWRITING THE EASY WAY

MARSH CASSADY

MERIWETHER PUBLISHING LTD.
Colorado Springs, Colorado

Meriwether Publishing Ltd., Publisher
P.O. Box 7710
Colorado Springs, CO 80933

Editor: Theodore O. Zapel
Cover design: Tom Myers

© Copyright MCMXCV Meriwether Publishing Ltd.
Printed in the United States of America
First Edition

Library of Congress Cataloging-in-Publication Data

Cassady, Marsh, 1936-
 Characters in action : playwriting the easy way / by Marsh Cassady.
  p. c.m.
 ISBN 1-56608-010-X (paper)
 1. Playwriting. I. Title.
PN1661.C37   1995
808.2—dc20   95-7721
                                                              . CIP

To Bill Jarosin and Pat Nakayama

Acknowledgements

Thanks to Jim Kitchen for his help in preparing this book.

The sample page of a script was written by Pat Cassady.

Excerpts from various sketches and character interviews by Marsh Cassady, used by permission of the author. Excerpts from specific works by Marsh Cassady, used by permission of the author: *The Monologue, One Moment in Time, NHI: No Human Involved; Scars; McGregor and the Wild Hares; At the Office, Nothing's Too Good for my Son, Surprise Party* (originally published in *By Kids for Kids*, edited by Catherine Gaffigan, New York: Excalibur Publishing, 1994), *Martin's Monologue* from *Tongues of Men and Angles, Brad and Frank* scene from *Double Occupancy.*

Excerpts from *Carwash* and *An Avalanche of Tenors* by Louis Phillips, used by permission of the author. *Carwash* originally appeared in *Crazyquilt Quarterly*, September 1989, and *An Avalanche of Tenors* in *The Hawaii Review*, Vol. 15, (Spring 1991).

Excerpts from *Marching in Time* and *Death by Stages* by Zachary Thomas and used by permission of the author.

Contents

Introduction

Throughout the years I've collected and developed the ideas included in this book both through my own writing and in various classes, seminars and workshops I've conducted for colleges, writing groups and a professional theatre.

Because of this, I've seen time and again that if a person follows the suggestions included in the first few chapters, it is a painless process to come up with ideas that can be developed into a play.

It is developing the ideas into a one-act or full-length play that is the more difficult task. However, even that is not so difficult if a writer keeps in mind that the two most important aspects of a script are character and conflict.

A writer also needs to remember that a play lacks meaning unless it is given focus, a reason for being, beyond that of entertainment. So even if it is begun in an artificial way, somewhere early on in its development, the playwright needs to examine why he or she is writing, and what the play means.

Although, of course, entertainment is the primary function of most drama, I feel a play should communicate something important to an audience. It should be more than "fluff." That is why the first section of the book talks about background in a person's life that may serve as a basis for a play, and why later there is a section on developing theme or central idea.

No playwright should attempt to write for the theatre without knowing about the theatre—that is, without having practical experience in as many areas as possible and direct observation in others.

It is also important to think of the audience, and to think of the reasons for wanting to write. That is why I have included sections both on analyzing an audience and on the various genres of theatre.

I believe too that except as an exercise for a beginning playwright and for practice in learning to develop characters, ideas, conflict and scenes, there is no good reason for writing without a market or audience in mind. So the final chapter provides information on ways you can go about having your play produced or published.

If you are serious about writing plays, read widely in all genres of literature, including drama. Read, read, read. See all sorts of plays from those presented by high schools and colleges to community theatre to regional to all the various types of professional theatre you can find.

Work in theatre as often and as much as you can. Work on productions of various sorts. Then find some good playwriting workshops or seminars and attend them.

CHAPTER 1

Germination

Where do plays come from?

They come from the playwright's vision.

When playwrights conceive ideas, these ideas are uniquely the writers'. Even so-called documentary plays are both more and less than the history they portray. The playwright, by choosing and eliminating, is therefore editing, adding a perspective.

If the subject of a play is a recent war, the playwright's feelings about that war will be unique. One person may choose to deal with the suffering of children who've seen their parents killed. Another may choose to deal with individual heroism, another to show war's folly.

Which idea is better? Who's to say? A real value judgment can be made only on the basis of how well the playwright succeeded in transferring the vision to paper and how well this written script translated into a production.

A play is incomplete in itself; its vision has to be shared. Theatre is collaboration.

But this is far along in the process.

First, there has to be a play.

So again, where do plays come from?

They come from vision and imagination. What is the basis of this vision and imagination? Ah, there is the crux of the matter. Each playwright, each person who wants to write for the theatre, has a different muse, a different perspective, a different starting point.

What are these starting points?

Some writers get their ideas from newspapers and other listings of current events and then start asking themselves questions about what they've read.

One morning three years ago I woke up in my apartment to hear helicopters circling, police radios blaring, and people talking outside my bedroom window.

By the time I was ready to leave for the downtown office where at that time I did my writing, most of the vehicles and people had dissipated.

The manager of the office building also lived in my apartment house. As soon as I walked through the front door and headed down the hall to my office, he cornered me. "Did you hear about the murder this morning?" he asked.

He went on to tell me how two men, roommates, had gotten into an argument and one had stabbed and cut the other repeatedly. "The living room walls, and the furniture" he said, "were stained red with blood."

Later accounts told how the murderer, in his early twenties, was so overwrought by what he had done that he drove in his car for hours, finally going into a bar in a nearby city. A customer asked him what was wrong.

The young man told how he and the other man had an argument over what to have for a dinner which they planned to share. The argument escalated, and ended with the other man's death.

The gist of the bar encounter was that the customer agreed to accompany the young man to the police station where he confessed what he'd done. Hours later then, several police cruisers and two helicopters (I really don't quite understand why!) showed up in my neighborhood.

Newspaper accounts told of the lives of both the murderer and the victim. The victim worked at a nearby hospital; the murderer was a student.

From this came my idea for my play, *One Moment in Time*. Because of "one moment in time" both lives, in effect, were ended.

I hoped to show that a single moment of anger and rashness defined two people entirely. It didn't matter what had gone before in their lives. Nothing mattered anymore, not their inter-

4

ests, abilities, talents, worries, passions, families, or concerns. Everything boiled down to one moment.

The two men were gay. But the murderer could just as well have been a heterosexual man murdering his wife or lover. It could have been a woman murdering a man, one lesbian murdering another.

One Moment in Time, I decided, would be about four couples, two of them straight, one gay and the other lesbian. I'd examine their lives, show their different sides, their personalities. There would be only eight cast members, each playing people from the past lives of all the others, as well as their major role of victim or murderer. My theme, my central idea would be that people, no matter what their backgrounds, sexual orientations, or dreams, can destroy themselves in a single rash moment.

My idea came from the "news"; it came from living next door to a murderer and his victim. It came from knowing, when I was a boy, a man I admired very much, a man who spent time with his own kids and other people's kids, who ten years later shot and killed his wife, one of his two children, and his mother, in an instant of rage or insanity.

I drew on what I knew, took a certain perspective on it— the tragedy of wasted or interrupted lives; the losing of control—to show that it doesn't matter what a person is throughout an entire life; it is one moment that can outweigh everything else. And it is by this single moment that the person thereafter is defined.

How does a playwright start? There are many ways. Here are a few you might try if you do not already have an idea for a play. In later chapters, we'll examine specific ways to come up with ideas.

1. Analyze what is important in your life. Take one of these things that interests you and examine why it's important. Is it important enough to want to bring to a theatre audience?

Of course, this means then that the play begins with a theme or a message:

a. The United States' above-ground testing of the atom bomb in the 1950s at best showed a laxity in announcing or enforcing safety precautions for citizens of Utah and Nevada, and at worst showed a total disregard for human lives.

b. Racial and ethnic prejudice is immoral.

c. "Above all, to thine own self be true."

Here are some things in which you believe—some more specific than others. But how are you going to present any of them in a play? In the first instance, you can trace the lives of a family who lived in a small town in Nevada and how one by one they began to die. Even though they tried to seek help, the government ignored their pleas and arguments. You can't write about people in general who died of leukemia and other forms of cancer as a result of the tests. You need specifics to express universal truths and so your audience can empathize and identify with individuals. For only in identifying with individuals can an audience truly care.

Or maybe you want to approach the idea differently. You might then take one of the top military officers involved with the project and have him see what really is happening, and show how he is frustrated and his career ruined when he tries to prevent it.

The point is that once you pick something that is important to you, you can approach it in many, many different ways. The play you write to illustrate your beliefs or theme will be different from anyone else's.

The second theme and the third, because they are less specific, could be expressed in even more ways. For instance, two black women playwrights dealt with the theme of racial prejudice in entirely different ways in *Aftermath* (a one-act by Mary Burrill) and *A Raisin in the Sun* (Lorraine Hansberry). The former is about a returning World War I soldier who learns that his father has been lynched and decides to get revenge; the latter is about the Younger family who are approached with bribe money not to move into an all-white neighborhood.

If you choose to deal with a particular theme, however, you need to take care that your play doesn't become just a soapbox.

6

It has to involve characters and a plot that make the audience members care. Otherwise, they might just as well have gone to hear a speech on the courthouse steps.

If you start with a theme, make sure you have characters and a situation that also are entertaining. Otherwise, you risk limiting your potential audience to those who believe in the same thing you do, rather than having any sort of chance of convincing others. Even if your major purpose is to point out something you think is wrong or something that should be changed, you have a better chance of convincing an audience you're right if you do it in an entertaining way.

Writing a play is not an overnight process, so do choose as the subject something that truly matters to you.

2. Similarly, you can begin a play by examining your feelings, by being honest in your approach to the subject.

This is similar to Activity #1, except that it may initially result in more introspection, in making you think more clearly about the sort of person you are and what affects you.

Does the theme or the subject really matter to you? Why? How do you really feel about the atom-bomb testing? Do you really care about what happened all those decades ago?

In a short play, *American Tropical*, by Richard Ford, a young woman tries to understand why she murdered someone. In my play, *One Moment in Time*, I try to examine why a basically decent person would murder someone else. Not only is this an examination of the specific case, but it is a questioning of what in general might cause one human being to murder another. So the play has much broader implications than the few cases it portrays.

In the one-act *FOB*, Henry Hwang looks at the clash between Chinese and American cultures. He examines what can happen to different sorts of first- or second-generation Americans who live in one culture at home and are thrust into another at school or in the world outside their home or neighborhood.

Hwang tries to be honest in his approach; he comes across as genuinely wanting to examine the issues. He draws no particular conclusions other than that such a clash creates problems

7

for those involved and how this affects them, even to the extent of their trying to deny what they are.

If you don't believe, as Anatol Fugard does, for instance, in *Master Harold and the Boys*, that there is a problem with apartheid, don't attempt to write about it.

This isn't to say that every play has to be strong in message. It doesn't. In all probability, Neil Simon wrote most of his earlier plays largely to be entertaining. Yet they do have something important to say. *Barefoot in the Park*, for instance, is about the need to compromise in order to get along in life. *Broadway Bound*, though, also is entertaining, yet it is more serious in its approach.

Antonio Skármeta chose to write his play *Burning Patience* about the Chilean poet Pablo Neruda, but against a background of a wider story of the evils of a fascist government. The playwright wrote about something important to him personally.

3. Choose to write about something that arouses your curiosity.

Choose something that interests you but you don't know much about. I've always been fascinated by a man named William Wells Brown, an escaped slave who never learned to read until he was an adult. I first encountered his name in the early 70s when I was researching the history of professional theatre in a small Ohio city. A newspaper, *The Anti-Slavery Bugle*, published in this city in the 1840s, announced that Brown would be appearing at Town Hall, performing in a play he'd written.

When my particular research was finished, I dug out all I could find on Brown. I discovered that despite his early beginnings, he became America's first black playwright, first black novelist, and first black travel writer; was a delegate to the International Peace Conference in Paris; was a historian, an attorney, a lecturer, an anthologist and possibly a physician.

Over the years I've done a lot of research on him, have written three articles about his life and presently am working on both a young adult biography and a play. Why was he such a super-achiever? What pushed him? What compelled him to excel in so many different areas, particularly with the sort of beginning he had? Why now is he essentially ignored by historians and history instructors?

Or take the short one-character play, *Rupert's Birthday* by Ken Jenkins, which examines how one particular incident in a girl's childhood, helping to birth a calf, strongly affected her entire life thereafter. In all probability, Jenkins wanted to examine how a particular event or series of events can have such a long-lasting effect.

In many ways, a play sets up a situation and then says "what if..." What if a few high school girls stop in at a restaurant and see an older man staring at them? What if they become uncomfortable, and one of them decides she has to know why he's staring? And what if she's wearing an old high school letter jacket that she picked up at a thrift store? And what if this jacket had belonged to the man's son? And what if the son is dead? How then would this affect the girl's and the man's lives?

This is exactly what happens in Mark O'Donnell's poignant one-act *Fables for Friends*, first presented in the mid-1980s in New York.

A playwright is curious, not only about specific things, but about what would happen if certain circumstances were established and characters were placed in these circumstances.

4. Similarly, choose a subject or a situation that is haunting.

Often it's a matter of wanting to make peace with something in your past. Sometimes it's wanting to set something straight. It can be something entirely personal or something much broader in its effects. For instance, Tennessee Williams based much of his writing on his sister. One of the characters he developed as a result of being haunted by what she had been and continued to be was the frail Laura in *The Glass Menagerie*. Arthur Miller was haunted by the McCarthy hearings and so used the analogy of a witch hunt in his play *The Crucible*.

Sometimes it takes years to write about such events because they are so close, so emotional that they affect us too strongly to examine them objectively. Yet often they are worth later effort in shaping the memories of them into plays.

The past shapes us, makes us what we are, and so is important to us. As I said, part of my reason for wanting to write *One Moment in Time* is that one of my favorite people from my teenage years was a man who later shot his family.

I was friends with his kids, knew and liked his wife and his mother. For me, it was the greatest sort of tragedy.

There are more personal tragedies as well. Robert Mauro's one-act play *I Never Said Goodbye* deals with being haunted by the past by showing what happens when a girl never said goodbye to a friend who died.

In *Letters to a Student Revolutionary*, Elizabeth Wong contrasts the lives of a young American woman of Chinese extraction and a young Chinese woman caught up in the events of the massacre of hundreds of Chinese students in the 1980s in Beijing's Tianamen Square. The playwright examines a casual relationship between the American and the woman she meets while on vacation in China. The encounter is brief, yet the two women keep in touch by letter. The play implies that the Chinese woman dies during the massacre.

It's probably safe to assume that Wong was haunted by what had happened and tried to understand or to make sense out of it.

The following, titled *The Monologue*, deals with another kind of haunting.

SETTING: The action takes place on an empty stage. SARAH, 17, is standing Down Center. She is neatly dressed, as if for an audition.

SARAH: Hi, I'm Sarah Walker. Why did I say that? You know that already. This is the first time I've ever auditioned. Professionally, I mean. For an actual role. School plays, church, things like that, I auditioned, but never — I'm sorry, I already said that.

   You want me to tell you about myself. God, I don't know what to tell you. I'm seventeen. I graduated from the school of performing arts last month — Oh, yeah, I guess I did audition professionally. I mean I was in the chorus of a musical. But that hardly counts, does it? Nearly everyone in my class was in the chorus of that musical. And it closed after one night. It closed after half a night. Everyone walked out. Right in the middle of a number. Like a trail of ants. They trickled right out. And there we were, singing and dancing and ...

10

I was born...I mean, this might be interesting. I was born in Liechtenstein. There aren't many foreigners born in Liechtenstein. Not many people born in Liechtenstein.

See, my parents were on this trip, and I was born early, and I was born in...

I came home when I was a week old. To British Columbia. Maybe I should explain that. My dad was working in British Columbia. I mean I'm not Canadian. Not that there's anything wrong with being Canadian. I'm not a Liechtenstinian eith — is that the word? Liechtenstinian?

Sorry, I'm babbling.

Mom said she thought I started performing the day I was born. She was just kidding, of course, but I can't remember when I didn't want to be an actress. Oh, God, I thought. It would be so wonderful. To be someone else, to be anyone else, to be a lot of other — I didn't want to be me. Never wanted ...

So anyhow I was always singing and dancing and reciting nursery rhymes. My mom says I knew the whole *"Night Before Christmas"* when I was a year and a half. A year and a half old, can you imagine? I'd say it at the drop of a pin. That's not right. Drop of a hat. That's right; that's what it is. Isn't it?

So anyhow I started singing and reciting poems and things in school and church and family reunions— I was never nervous. You might think I'm nervous. But I was never nervous. High-strung like a thoroughbred. That's what Dad said. He didn't know anything about horses. Never even saw a race. That's what he told me.

You're letting me babble on here. *(Laughs nervously.)* So maybe I could recite something. How about it? What do you say? Can I recite something?

Nah, I better not. You want to hear about my life. Well, there's nothing important. I grew up in — Oh, yeah, I used to play the accordion. Squeeze box is what Grandma called it. *(Broadly pantomimes playing an accordion.)*

Bagpipes. That's what I thought the accordion sounded like. Don't ask me why. Same principle, I guess. Air squeezed in and out to make the sound. Bagpipes are always so, I don't know so...so mournful. Like the cry of a lonely siren *(Caught up in the mood)* luring sailors to deep, vast graves in the sea.

(Snapping out of it) But you don't want to hear about bagpipes; you know about bagpipes. The whole world knows about bagpipes. Maybe not the whole world.

(Takes a deep breath and expels it.) Where was I? Oh, yeah, so I grew up in Jersey. Newark. Can you imagine growing up in Newark? I didn't really grow up in Newark. I moved here when I was thirteen. I mean when I found out about the school of performing arts, and that the kids there got to audition for shows. Professional shows. Wow, you know. Anyhow, I came to stay with my grandma. And I went home weekends, except when I was in a *(exaggerated French accent)* tragédie ou comédie ou a lettle chanson ou danse nombair. *(Serious)* I didn't really want to go home. It was so strange going home. Back into all that — Back into everything — I mean like Mom never even said any—

I'm making a fool of myself up here. Isn't that what I'm doing? Making a fool of myself. Well, so what? You wanted to hear me talk; you wanted to hear me sing and act. Did you want to hear me sing?

I don't have any brothers and sisters. Mom says who could put up with another one like me? She was just kidding...I think. *(Laughs and points straight ahead.)* Of course, she was kidding. *(Serious again)* Except I know she and Dad would have been much happier if — I didn't ask them to be born, did I? And then the way he — I mean, nobody deserves to be tr—

(Brightly) Say, don't I get to read or something? Oh, yeah, the paper you handed me. *(She pantomimes looking at a sheet of typing paper.)* When I'm done telling you about myself, I'm supposed to read it, act it. But am I done telling you about myself? I mean, I'm done telling you about myself if you want me to be done telling you about myself. But, I can...Oh, well.

Yes, now. I see. It's on the paper here. You told me my audition piece was on the paper here. Nothing prepared, you said. A cold reading. Right here on the paper. Okay, here we go. Here it is. *(Reading from the imaginary paper, almost to herself)* "To be or not to be." Oh sure I know that. Everyone knows that. Doesn't everyone know that? *(Reciting in broad Shakespearean tones)* "To be or not to be, that is the question. Whether 'tis nobler in the mind to suffer the slings and arrows of outrageous for—" Hey! Wait a minute here. This is Hamlet. This is a boy. I mean, not a boy, but a man. A young man. Maybe not a boy; he is in college, I think. Isn't he? A college boy. Man. Isn't Hamlet in college somewhere? Sweden, Denmark, something like — Oh, yeah, of course, he's *from* Denmark. He's Danish. Danish? How do you get Danish out of Den — Lochtenstunian! Maybe that's what I'd be if we hadn't come home. To British Columbia. To Newark. To... Actually I don't know why they brought me home. They never wanted — And so—anyhow, I was glad to live with Grandma. I had to get away. Oh, God.

Hey, wait! Whoa! Hold everything. The fine print. I see the fine print here. *(Quoting from the imaginary paper from which she'd been reading)* This company was founded for the purpose of expanding gender and ethnic roles.

(Puzzled) A Dane is ethnic? So what am I? Aren't I ethnic already? I mean besides the way I look. See the way I look. And you have me playing a Danish white boy? I mean, hey, like they used to say, get with it! Ooh, sorry, I didn't mean anything. Wow, if I say stuff like that—I mean, if I keep on saying stuff like that, I'm really going to blow it, aren't I?

So shall we try it again? "To be or not—" Expanding our views and our roles, is that it? You know I kind of admire that. No, really, I mean I do. I really admire that.

So, hey, should I try a little dance step? Why don't I try a little dance step? *(Doing the chorus line bit)* One and a two and a one and a two and a — Remember Lawrence Welk? Oh, God when I was a little kid, I used to sit in front of the TV set when the "Lawrence Welk Show" came on. I wanted so bad to be one of those sisters, what were their names? You know, the sisters who sang and all that stuff on the "Lawrence Welk Show"? I envied them so much. And Patty Duke. Remember her as a little girl with her own TV show? And those old movies? Shirley Temple and Margaret O'Brien. I'd give anything if I could have had a life that was just a little bit like — that was normal, damn it!

Sorry. I'm really sorry. You don't want to hear that kind — I mean, oh, wow, you've just got to know how important this is to me. It's really important. More important than food and sleeping and...well, you know, don't you? Sure, you know, it's like the most important thing in the whole wor — Not really the most important. Grandma—well both Grandmas. And Grandpa ...

(Mock serious) I never knew my one Grandpa. Now don't get the wrong idea. He didn't die or anything. He was one of those astronauts who went to the moon. The one you never heard about, the one they all kept quiet about. It was my grandpa. Went to the moon. A young man. And he liked the moon. And so he decided to live on the moon. *(Trying to keep from laughing)* No, really, my grandpa's alive. Both grandmas and grandpas. It's really my uncle who lives on the moon. *(Laughs)*

My grandma was a singer. Mom's mom, and Grandpa played guitar. That's how they met. Isn't that romantic? Now isn't it? And it's the truth.

My other grandma plays the piano. Grandpa isn't musical though. He collects stamps.

So where was I? Oh, sure. A one and a — Nah! You don't want to see me dance. You want me to recite something? What? What can I recite? I know.

(Very hammy) "It was many and many a year ago
In a kingdom by the sea.
There lived a maid whom you may know
 by the name of...Sara Lee?"

14

Funny. *(Almost pleading)* Isn't that funny? You see, that's my name. Sarah Lee, with an "H." Sarah Lee Walker. *(Parody of a western movie)* So, what do you think about that, pardner?

(Her normal voice) Are you just going to let me die up here? I don't mean really die. I mean die like in doing a terrible job, not knowing what to say or do. Or—

I got an idea. I'll tell you about my hobbies. *(Long pause)* I don't have any hobbies. The only thing I'm interested in is being an actress. That's my whole life's ambition. Everything else revolves around that. I'm being serious. I mean it. I know I've been kidding a lot, because, believe it or not, I didn't know what else to do. What else to say. But not now.

Why do people want to be actors or actresses? Why do I want to be an actress? I don't really know. It's just the most wonderful feeling in the world. Everybody watching and listening and the house so still you can hear a hat drop. *(Laughs and points.)* Got you again, didn't I!?

(Serious) No, but I mean it. It's not like I want to control people, or even that I feel I'm so important or special. *(Pause)* Even though I am. Important and special, I mean. Kidding. Just kidding.

(Serious again) It's like I'm this instrument playing a duet with...God maybe? Or the consciousness of the universe. And everything's aligned somehow. And I'm the chemical catalyst or the reed of a tenor sax or the sounding board of a piano. And if I've rehearsed and studied and am confident, well, it's like I'm playing and being played so the audience hears one pure, sweet note. Or a resounding chord.

(Changing abruptly) So you heard any good jokes lately? You'd think with my wanting to perform and loving to be up here on stage that I'd be pretty good at telling jokes. Well, I'm not. I always mess up the punch line. I forget it or something. I wonder why. I can say lines in a play just fine. Right intonation and emphasis. But I can't tell a joke. Maybe life itself's a joke. And

15

we're stuck with one role. I was stuck in one role. A role I hated, till I moved in with Grandma and Grandpa. Can a person be an actress just because her life is — because she wants to get away, to escape — God, I'm seventeen years old. Why did I want to escape? Why do I still want...to...escape? *(Tears in her eyes)* It was like Mom didn't care. She knew what was going on. What Dad was doing to me. But she just didn't—

(An abrupt change) So, hey, do I have the role or don't I? I mean, I feel like I've been up here forever, and I haven't said a blessed thing. Haven't done a blessed thing. I mean I was always good at ad libbing. When I was in junior high, before I went to the school of performing arts, I joined the speech club. You know, readings and contests and stuff. Well, I always did well with the impromptu event. Give me a subject, and whether I know anything or not about it, I can talk. I'll show you.

Give me anything to talk about, any subject. Say it's...quantum physics. All right? Ahem. Ahem. Good evening, ladies and gentlemen.

Quantum physics, huh? What made me think of quantum physics? I don't know what made me think of quantum physics. Black holes. That's it. Quantum physics and black holes.

(Orotund tones) Ladies and gentlemen, a discourse on black holes. What is a black hole, ladies and gentlemen? It's a hole in the sky. A hole in the sky that's black. Not brown, not green, not red. But black. Yes, people, it's black. And why is it black? Well, because...it isn't really there. It's somewhere else. It's in some other universe. Ha! Didn't think I knew that, did you? A tunnel to the future or the past. Anti-matter.

But you can't go through a black hole. If you tried to go through a black hole, it's hard to tell what would happen besides being crunched down so you'd cover only one billionth of a billionth of a pinhole...

So thank you, ladies and gentlemen. My mother thanks you; my father thanks you; my grandmother thanks you; my grandfather thanks you. *(Her voice trails off.)* All of them...*(Sadly)* That's dumb. Mom and Dad wouldn't thank...They wouldn't give a damn. But the big thing is that I'll be on my own, and Dad can't — *(Realizing what she's saying)* What am I saying! But if I can play at being someone else, at least for a while, I really can be that person, become that person, do you see? Everything's better. Everything's different. I'm different. And Dad can't do those horrible things anymore, and Mom can't pretend she doesn't know what — *(Panicky)* Oh, my God, I'm sorry. I shouldn't say things like — I'm...sorry.

(Brightly) So...what else would you like to know? *(Pause as if listening to a response)*

I can quit! I really can quit now. And I have the job. Oh, wow, I'll have to tell Grandma and Grandpa. And I'll tell Mo — *(Suddenly, she becomes dignified and composed, a young woman in command of her life.)* Thank you. Thank you very much. *(She nods and hurries Off-stage.)*

(CURTAIN)

The monolog is a play in itself where a young woman is trying to go past the effects of child abuse and make her life worthwhile.

In his book *The Dramatist's Toolkit*, playwright and play-writing instructor Jeffrey Sweet cautions that it often is difficult to write about your past life because people tend to view themselves as acted upon, rather than acting. A central character needs to act and react, and so if you cast yourself as the protagonist, you may be setting up the play as an instant failure.

Yet in the foregoing monolog, the writer takes something in the past and shows how it affects the character's actions still. Of course, in the situation of child abuse, the child is acted upon, or at least the implications are strong that her father sexually abused her. But the monolog doesn't go back to that period of time except in showing how it presently affects Sarah's life.

Obviously, this is a haunting experience; it influences everything Sarah does.

5. *Choose a person or a character upon whom to base a play.*

Often you can begin with a historical figure, such as Pablo Neruda, or William Wells Brown, or Helen Keller and Annie Sullivan (*The Miracle Worker*). Then the events — both macrocosmic or outside the person and microcosmic, inside and close to the person — determine in part the content of the play. Of course, how you, the playwright, view these events will determine your approach.

Or you can take someone you know, perhaps someone you greatly admire or maybe even someone you strongly dislike and explore both them and your reactions to them. What do you want to show about them? What are the most important aspects of their characters? Why do you want to write about them, and what is most important to say? And if it is important to you, will it or can it be equally important to others?

Think of present friends and acquaintances or people from your past and determine their most outstanding qualities.

To show these — greediness, for instance, or selflessness — you need to place the character in situations and settings in which you can explore the traits. Then you need other characters with whom they can react to show what you want to show about them.

Use the person you know or knew as a starting point. Even if you tried to transfer him or her to a play and subsequently to the stage, it would be impossible because your perceptions color the situation you remember. In all probability, the longer the time since you knew the person, the more your remembrance is colored.

The point is, don't try to transfer real people whom you know to the stage. Rather take certain traits and heighten them, point them up, choose best how to explore these traits.

Moliére is said to have done this, using himself as a model, for *The Imaginary Invalid*.

In a later chapter, there will be much more on developing characters.

6. *You can begin with a set of circumstances.*

This is most certainly what the playwright Charles Kray did with *A Thing of Beauty*, set in Nazi Germany and telling the story

18

of a Jewish woman, Edith Stein, who has become a Carmelite nun, Sister Benedicta.

Although concerned with the problem of Nazi domination and persecution before and during World War II, the play focuses on Sister Benedicta and a Nazi colonel caught up in the events of the time.

You can take any set of circumstances and build characters and a plot from there. David Storey probably did this with his play *Home*, about inmates of a mental hospital.

Tina Howe used both the circumstances and her memories (hauntings) of her parents in her play *Painting Churches*, where the action takes place as the mother and father are moving out of a house in which they've lived for years.

7. Begin with a setting.

Poet, novelist and playwright Louis Phillips might easily have done this with his comedy *Carwash* in which vehicles driven through the Charm School Carwash fail to come out the other side. Here is a brief excerpt:

DARLENE: What seems to be the trouble here?
PFEIFFER: I want the manager.
DARLENE: I am the manager.
PFEIFFER: Of course. Everybody's a manager in this business.
    It's something you learned from the Japanese.
DARLENE: What's that supposed to mean?
JOE: He's upset because he lost his car.
DARLENE: He lost his car?
JOE: He lost his car.
PFEIFFER: I lost my car.
DARLENE: You lost your car?
PFEIFFER: What are we talking about here?
JOE: I thought we were talking about losing your car.
PFEIFFER: That's right. That's exactly what I'm talking
    about. Losing my car.
DARLENE: If you lost your car, what are you doing at a car-
    wash? It doesn't make any sense to come to a carwash
    without any car.
PFEIFFER: Are you crazy? What are you talking about? I
    came here with my car. And now I don't have a car. I

put it in there. *(Points to the carwash tunnel.)*
DARLENE *(to JOE)*: What's he talking about?
JOE: He lost his car.
DARLENE: He lost his car?
PFEIFFER: I lost my car...in there.
DARLENE: Is this some kind of a joke? You lost your car in there?
PFEIFFER: I didn't lose the car. You lost the car.
DARLENE *(to JOE)*: What's he talking about? It's impossible to lose a car in there.
PFEIFFER: You did something to it.
JOE: I didn't touch the car.
PFEIFFER: Somebody touched the car!
JOE: I don't touch the cars until they come out of the tunnel. Your car didn't come out of the tunnel. Therefore, I didn't touch it.

You might begin such a play by going to a carwash and wondering what mysterious things actually happen as the car slowly advances through the washing, scrubbing, rinsing and drying off. Hence you have a comedy in which the physical laws of the universe are suspended, at least for a time, and matter disappears entirely with no logical explanation.

One of my recent audio plays began with seeing homeless people taking partially empty cartons of food from city trash cans. What, I wondered, would happen if these cartons of food were to contain poison?

Why would anyone want to poison the homeless seemingly at random? Well, suppose it wasn't at random. Suppose someone was only making it appear that way to confuse the authorities about the real target?

What sort of person would do that? Why? Who would be the intended victim, and what could this person have done that so enraged someone that he would have no qualms about killing innocent people just to get back at him?

My play is called *NHI: No Human Involved*, taken from the callous attitude some have that street people, prostitutes, and gang members are somehow sub-human.

8. Adapt a play from another medium.

There have been many plays adapted from novels and biographies or even from collections of stories. The only problem here is that you have to be sure you have permission from the copyright holder or author to draw on the material for your play.

Many plays like this have become very successful. The play *Porgy* was adapted by Dubose and Dorothy Heyward from Dubose Heyward's novel *Porgy*. This in turn was adapted into the musical version *Porgy and Bess* by George Gershwin.

Martin Duberman's play *In White America*, which is the history of the persecution of blacks in the U.S. from slave times to the present, is a documentary drama drawing on diaries, interviews, articles and newspapers.

There are literally hundreds of plays adapted from other mediums.

If none of these methods of beginning a play appeals to you, Chapter 3 contains a number of more "artificial" methods of beginning.

Perhaps you've already discovered that getting ideas is not a problem, once you gear yourself to look for them. Rather, the problem is choosing which of the many ideas appeals to you most.

ACTIVITIES

1. Read a newspaper or watch a TV newscast with the idea of coming up with an idea you can use as a basis for a play. Begin to develop your idea. If you are using this book as part of a class, share the idea with your fellow students. In the process, try to refine it and build characters, a setting, a situation and a storyline.

2. Jot down five or ten things that are important to you and your life. Then think about why they are important. Maybe you can develop an idea based on one of them to share with the rest of your class. Talk about one of these things. Decide if this is something you would want to share with a theatre audience. If it is, think about how you can bring this belief or idea to an audience in an entertaining way.

21

3. Examine your feelings as related to certain issues. Why do you feel as you do? Do other people feel the same way? Remember that a play does not have to deal with anything totally new. It simply can reinforce old beliefs or values by calling attention to them.

Decide what values or beliefs are important enough to you to want to share them and point them up for an audience. Then begin to develop characters, a setting and circumstances where you can explore these in a play.

4. What are you curious about? Is there anything you've read or heard about or some person or event your family members or friends have discussed that you want to understand more fully? Or are you particularly drawn to any historical events or personages? Why are you? If you are interested or curious about them, maybe others will be too. Even if they aren't, how can you make them curious?

5. Is there something that keeps haunting you, that you can't let go? Why did that acquaintance of yours commit suicide? Why did your best friend quit high school in the middle of your junior year? What really is involved in becoming a good musician or painter, and why are some people driven to excel in these areas?

Investigate one of these areas further, or take a "what if" approach. What if someone had spent time talking with the acquaintance who committed suicide? What could have been done, if anything, to prevent this from happening? How can you make this into a compelling or entertaining play?

Almost any subject or occurrence or person can provide the basis for a play. You just need to figure out how to approach them.

6. Who is a character whom you admire, who has accomplished a great deal, who is antisocial, who is despicable? What made the person this way? Why does the person continue in this vein?

Writing is the art of asking questions and answering them. If the play you want to write is entirely based in fact, stick to primary and secondary sources — interviews, books, articles — and so on in your investigation. If you use a person as only a starting point, take the life or the situation further in your imagination.

7. Develop a set of circumstances into a concrete idea for a play. At your job or at your school, you discover cheating or dishonesty. Who is involved? Why are they involved? What will be the results of this? How will this affect the person and others connected to him or her?

Take any set of circumstances and build from there, using what you know as the basis and projecting the rest with the "what if" approach.

8. Observe a place and see in your imagination what happens there. Maybe it's a ghetto where gangs rule. How does this affect the people there? How does it affect one specific person? Who is this person? Why is the person important? Will he or she try to do something to improve things? What? What will be the result? How will this result affect others?

CHAPTER 2
The Creative State

PRODUCER: Okay then, a complete rewrite, understood. And I need it by tomorrow morning. I mean, gee, buddy, that first act sucks, and the second's no better. And we don't even have a third — I mean, have you even started on it? Surely, you don't call what you gave me a third act. You know, like I got all these actors coming in here this afternoon, thinking they're gonna start rehearsing? So what's gonna happen? They're gonna stand around, doin' nothin', 'cause there's nothing to rehearse. You do understand what I'm saying, right?

PLAYWRIGHT: I, uh, er, uh, that is, I'll —

PRODUCER: I mean it, guy. You think I'm made of money? Well, think again. 'Cause if that script's not done, and done right —

PLAYWRIGHT: *(Drawing his knees up slowly to his chest)* I'll ... oh, God. I'll — Please, I'll — I'll do the best —

PRODUCER: Your best, huh? From what I've seen, that ain't so hot. Get with it man, understand me?

PLAYWRIGHT: *(Knees drawn up tight, his head sinking against his chest)* Uhhh, uhhh, uhhh, uhhh.

PRODUCER: What's your problem, bud? You're getting no sympathy with that kind of ... I mean, not from me, pal, okay? *(PLAYWRIGHT's eyes roll up inside his head; he falls sideways and topples off his chair.)*

DIRECTOR: I do believe he's gone catatonic, eh what?

PRODUCER: Yeah, and if he don't snap out of it, I'll see he never gets another script produced in this town —

DIRECTOR: Hey, did I ever tell you about my brother-in-law? Used to be an auto mechanic at Joe's Garage. Over on Fifth? Till he got himself fired. Fancies himself a writer. Pretty good too, if I say so myself. So what do you say? You do need a script. Frank needs a job. Say the word, and I'll give him a jingle ...

Of course, it's possible to create under many different circumstances, but unless we are relaxed and focused on the creation, it is much more difficult and probably will involve many false starts and stops.

25

It's much easier if we're in the proper frame of mind. This means, in effect, that we enter into an altered state of consciousness, a state in which we are so engrossed in the act of creation, so focused that little else intrudes upon our consciousness.

In times like this, we are more open to ideas. It's a common experience for writers to "record" things of which they felt they had no knowledge. It's a matter of learning to trust yourself and your abilities. I've found that when this sort of thing happens to me and I check it out, most often the information proves to be correct.

It's as if I can draw upon information that normally is so deeply buried that I have no conscious knowledge of it. Some people feel that because this sort of thing happens regularly in the midst of creating, in the altered state of consciousness we've entered, we somehow are in touch with the "cosmic consciousness," where ideas and knowledge not necessarily our own but part of the "cosmos" are there for the taking.

Others refer to the state as being in touch with a Higher Self. Whatever occurs, if we allow ourselves to enter the state with no restraints or reservations, things will occur that surprise us.

ERATO: So did you realize that amniocentesis was developed by two guys working independently? Independently, can you imagine? Of course, you can imagine. One of these guys was in Cleveland. Cleveland, Ohio not Cleveland National Forest in California. There aren't any research labs in Cleveland National Forest. Well, I mean there may be research labs, but no one in a research lab in —
PLAYWRIGHT: Will you shut up! Just please shut up!
ERATO: I'm a muse, man, it's my job to talk. I mean anything you want to know, I'll tell you. Anything you want to write about, just say it, any inspiration. Anything. Or if I don't know I'll ask someone. I got connections, know what I mean? Anyhow, where was I? Oh, yeah, it was the mid-seventies, thereabouts, and these two guys, one of them in Cleveland, Ohio, not Cleveland National Forest. I mean Cleveland, Ohio, is a

26

lot different than Cleveland National Forest —
WRITER: AAAAGH! I just want to write my haiku, my teeny, bitsy, little —
ERATO: Oh, yes, haiku, a Japanese art form. Basho? Remember Basho? What do you want to know about Basho? Anything you want to know about Basho, I'll tell you. And by the way, did you know that the haiku didn't start out just as the haiku? Oh, no, it started out as part —
WRITER: Why me? I don't understand, why me? The cosmic consciousness, the Higher Self. Other writers tell me about them. How wonderful they are. Beautiful ideas, like snowy feathers of downy birds, floating, floating, landing softly in their altered consciousness —
ERATO: Yes, I see, but as I was saying. What exactly was I saying? Oh, yes, I remember now. Basho. Haiku. The Japanese. Did you know the Japanese have Noh plays? Get it? Noh plays. Not no plays, but Noh plays? Isn't that funny? I mean —
WRITER: *(Tearing out big clumps of his hair, he dives through the window of this office, high above Gotham City.)* Peace, peace, wonderful peace. At last, there shall be peace. *(As he falls toward the sidewalk, the WRITER glances over and sees ERATO.)*
ERATO: Not polite, sir, not polite at all. I was talking to you about theatre, Japanese theatre. Theatre from the Orient, ancient theatre ...

It's common for a writer or a sculptor, for instance, to have a distorted sense of time because of being so deeply involved that an entire morning or afternoon can seem like a hour or two.

At these times of complete immersion into the creative state, an hour can seem like fifteen minutes, an afternoon, an hour. And because we are so attuned to what we are doing, we block out everyday concerns and worries. Then there is a feeling of joyfulness, particularly after we come back to the mundane world.

When my kids were still at home, they knew that unless it was a dire emergency, they were not to interrupt Dad while he was writing. This is because when I (or anyone else) am in a deeply creative state, it's like being in another place entirely, another world from which I need to be called back.

I'm like a deep sea diver having to emerge through layers of water — or consciousness. Then once the creative state is broken, it often is difficult to return.

Entering the state may take time. It's like being hesitant to take the plunge into a swimming pool or pond because we know the water at first is cold. But once we're in, we enjoy it.

A COMMON BASE

I believe that there is a common base for creativity that applies to all the arts, most particularly to the verbal arts of writing, acting and storytelling. To a degree the preparations for entering the creative state for a playwright or novelist are the same as those for a sculptor or painter, for instance.

This commonality involves trust in ourselves and our abilities, a willingness — almost like being in the hands of a hypnotist — to alter consciousness. And once we are there, we feel the same sort of high a runner does when the endorphins kick in.

Some people, who practice their art regularly, can enter the creative state with little preparation. Sometimes, however, even for these people, outside forces intrude: worries about everyday things like having money to pay bills, ill health, and so on.

· The creative state involves "relaxed concentration." Although this may seem to be an oxymoron, it is not. It is much easier to concentrate fully and well on something when both our bodies and minds are relaxed.

PHYSICAL RELAXATION

I rarely engage in any long preparation anymore for entering the creative state because after years of acting, storytelling and writing, I find it has become much easier. However, there still are a few physical exercises I do to become relaxed. There are many you can figure out for yourself, keeping in mind that these are not the sort of exercises designed to build stamina or muscles.

One that I always do is neck rolls. Each of us, when we stop to examine how we feel, in all probability will feel tension in various places in our bodies. I always feel most tension in my neck and shoulders.

So to relax, I gently roll my head clockwise over my shoulders, back and chest, and then reverse directions. If you try this, do it in each direction no more than two or three times or you may begin to feel dizzy.

Another favorite of mine is simply to stretch. Always before I perform in front of an audience and often before I sit down to write, I stretch one leg out in front of me, slightly bent at the knee, while I stretch the other leg in back. Then I bounce very gently for a few seconds before reversing legs; that is, placing the one that was in back in front and bent at the knee and the other back. For me, this is the most relaxing exercise there is. Others may work better for you.

Another exercise involves yawning, standing on tiptoe, and stretching your arms toward the ceiling. After this, stretch your arms out at your sides and in front. All of these shouldn't take more than a minute or two, and they can make a big difference in how you feel.

MENTAL RELAXATION

There are also ways of relaxing mentally. Some people find it helpful to meditate before beginning to write. This can help clear the mind of petty concerns and allow you to concentrate on developing a scene or a character.

This can be formal meditation where you say a mantra or listen to tapes. But there are other ways as well. I have a few different techniques that work for me; they involve engaging in various fantasies. So if the following sorts of things work for you, that's fine. If not, you can easily design some of your own.

The most relaxing for me is to think of my grandfather's farm which I visited every Sunday as a boy. Often I simply roamed the fields and woods. But I had two favorite spots. The first was a stream with ice cold water. At the place in the stream where I spent most of my time, branches stretched across the water leaving dappled patterns of sunlight and shadow on the earth and water.

I haven't visited the stream in decades. But often to relax, I imagine myself sitting on the bank, taking off my shoes and socks and dangling my feet in the water, letting soft silt flow around my feet and sift through my toes.

Or I imagine walking in the "sugar woods," a stand of maple trees, cleared of all undergrowth and blanketed with layers of humus and newly fallen leaves. Sometimes as I walk, in my imagination, through this place, or as I sit on the bank of the stream, I envision two or three deer standing on a knoll off in the distance.

Or sometimes I imagine myself a crow soaring high above the earth. Everything below, including any problems or concerns I have, is small and remote. I feel the sun on my wings, the gentle currents of air that take me over fields and forests and towns.

DEVELOPING SENSITIVITY

In order to create more easily, you need to become attuned to your surroundings and to other people. You need to learn to see things in new ways, to experience life through new points of view. Like the fantasies I mentioned, there are many ways in which you can do this.

One is to pretend to perceive things as if you've never witnessed them before, or as if you'll never witness them again and want to remember them.

Look at friends or family members as if this is the first time you've seen them, and then describe them as completely as possible in a character sketch you write.

Observe people you see on the street, at work, at school. Really pay attention not only to the way they look, but to how they talk and carry themselves and how this is different from the way anyone else does these things.

This is useful not only for writing but for such things as acting, giving readings, and telling stories.

Some people find it useful to keep a sort of journal about others — including notes they jot down describing nuances of speech, ways of gesturing, things you can observe about their approach to any task or relationship. I have a writer friend who keeps scrapbooks of pictures she's cut from magazines. To get inspiration, she leafs through these, surmising what an individual is like, based on clothing, hair style, jewelry and physical appearance.

Get into the habit of trying to see life through other's eyes. How would the old man who lives down on the corner view life differently from the way the young mother does who lives next door to you? Take the exercise even further. After carefully observing these people, go through an hour, a morning or a day assuming their characters, pretending you are one of them.

How do your perceptions differ now? How do you feel differently now about your neighborhood, the other people there? What bothers you as this person that doesn't bother you as yourself? How do your goals, your needs, your wants differ from those of your own self?

Watch people for a few moments, and on the basis of what you observe, make projections about what they are like or what they are feeling.

For instance, you see a woman's face in a passing bus. She's in her early thirties and she looks sad or upset. Why? Put yourself into her place, at least as the basis for your imagining. Maybe she's just lost her job and her husband is recovering from surgery and can't work. Maybe she's been turned down for a job with the town's leading dance company. How does this affect her? How does she feel about herself? How would another type of person feel differently about these same situations? Analyze why you've come to certain conclusions.

WRITER: *(Reflecting on a man he saw in the post office)* **The hands. Somehow they were the most important part; knotted, twisted, covered with veins. The suit, nondescript, a carry-over from the old country, from wherever he'd lived his earlier life.** *(Smiles in remembrance.)* **Flannel shirt with a tie, old brown cap, weathered face. I remember those things. But ... it's the hands that call attention — skin like the outside of an onion or a rose left too long in the sun — two hands. Shaking, clutching, tearing at the envelope, the envelope with the foreign stamp.**

31

Go out walking or to a store or mall. Observe one or two people. Then come back home and write a thumbnail sketch, including both physical and personality traits. Get into the habit of really seeing, of really paying attention. Make notes of what you see, adding your feelings and perceptions:

Supermarket parking lot after the rain; Vietnamese woman, black hair blowing. On her back, a baby bound with a quilt. For an instant, from out of this asphalt parking lot, steaming jungles grow.

This sort of observation and recording holds true for other things as well, not necessarily as an end in itself, but as a preparation for creating a setting, a set of circumstances.

Try to see something new on a route that you travel everyday. Maybe there's a particular tree you've never seen before. What makes it different? Why does it now capture your attention? Pay attention to buildings and lawns and gardens.

Walk into an unfamiliar place, a courthouse, a room in a library, a section of a museum. Try to memorize as much about the place as you can. Leave and then record all you can remember about the place — the type of architecture, the walls and floors and ceilings, the objects in the room. When you've finished, revisit the place and determine all that you've missed. Now go to a different place and do the same thing, constantly trying to remember more and more about each subsequent location.

When you go back to your house or apartment, do the same. Look around one of the rooms, leave, and then record everything that you saw. Go back later and see what you've missed.

A person has an easier time of writing by truly learning to see and hear and observe, because then there is more specific information to draw upon. Pay attention to everyday things, common experiences. What does it really feel like to walk outside in a gentle summer rain? How does the mist feel on your face? How does the earth smell? What do the streets and buildings and cars look like?

How is this different from being caught outside in a downpour? How does it affect you physically, emotionally? How would a character in a play feel about it? Take into consideration everything else that affects your own feelings on that particular day or afternoon, and that affects your character at the same time. Eugene O'Neill was a master at this sort of thing. For instance, read Edmund's monolog in Act Four of *Long Day's Journey Into Night* in which he talks about his feelings about the sea.

Try this sort of thing with any common experiences — climbing into a bed with newly laundered sheets or climbing into a lumpy bed in a second-rate hotel. How do these affect both physical and mental feelings?

Pay attention to the smell and taste of the food you eat. How is the texture of the outside of a piece of fruit different from the inside? How does the fruit taste or smell? How are these distinctive from other kinds of fruit? What is unique about them?

Exercise your memory — a good thing for any writer. Think of people, events, objects from your past. Call up details one by one and think about them; think how they affected you emotionally at the time. How do you feel about them now?

Spend time with each memory, till you can recall it clearly.

Try this: stop and really listen for ten or fifteen seconds and then write down the different sounds you heard. Now do this same exercise with a friend and compare lists. You'll probably be surprised at how many sounds you missed.

Learn to perceive as much as possible and then to transfer these perceptions to a character in a play. Pay attention to your emotions, to others' emotions. How do different people show the same feelings? How do you express anger differently than a friend does? Why do you think this is so? Obviously, it's your differences in personality and experience, but what specifically accounts for the way each of you exhibits anger? How would the character you are developing react in still a different way?

EXERCISING YOUR IMAGINATION

Watch people beginning some sort of task, delivering mail, scrubbing a floor, setting a table. Then in your imagination, take the person through the rest of the task. How would he or she do it differently than you would? How does the person move or carry himself or herself?

33

Learning to be creative involves an openness, a willingness, a freedom. Those who do the best jobs usually are the persons who are not afraid to give their imaginations free reign.

ACTIVITIES

1. Try to develop some exercises, both mental and physical, that will help you relax. If you are studying playwriting as part of a class, share these exercises with your fellow students, so that you have a larger base from which to draw in your own preparations for entering the creative state.

2. Develop a "fantasy" for helping you to relax, whether visiting a particular place in your mind, seeing a painting and placing yourself in the painting or some other way.

3. Write a half page to a page describing a building or the interior of a building you recently visited and with which you were not familiar.

4. Describe in detail a character getting caught in a heavy rain, having to wake up to go to work after a restless night, petting a kitten or a puppy.

5. Describe in detail a person you've observed performing a particular task. What physical movements were involved? How did this person's approach to the task differ from the way you or someone else might perform it?

6. Write a paragraph or two about something new that you observed today.

7. List as many new things as you can that you observed today in familiar locations.

Getting Ideas

There are any number of ways to get ideas for writing plays. But remember that ideas are only the beginning, the easy part.

THE CHARACTER INTERVIEW

The first way comes directly from an acting exercise. As originally intended, this was to help actors see that it is not difficult to develop a character, either for improvisation or from a written play.

You can use it one of two ways, to get ideas for a new character(s) and play, or to help you develop a character who is giving you trouble. I've done this with other people and with myself by playing both roles.

If you use it in a classroom, for instance, everyone except the interviewee can randomly ask questions. However, it works just as well with two people or even by yourself. In fact, I think it's an invaluable way to develop ideas.

There are three rules in doing a character interview.

1. You cannot plan anything out ahead of time.

2. The person being interviewed (or yourself if you are playing both roles) cannot answer as self but rather as an emerging character.

3. Everything the interviewee says has to be consistent with what has gone before. The person cannot, for example, both like and hate chocolate ice cream, be both thin and overweight, or basically be both stingy and generous. Of course, there can be cases where a stingy person is generous and vice versa, but not as a basic trait.

Simply let the questions and answers flow. That's what I just did with the following, which I started with no preconceived ideas about character, plot or situation. Except for minor editing to clean up punctuation and for the sake of clarity, I made no changes.

Q: **Who are you?**
A: **That should be pretty obvious, shouldn't it? I'm a damn**

prisoner in your stupid little country.

Q: In my stupid little country?

A: Pretty stupid for arresting me.

Q: Why were you arrested?

A: Look, is any of this important? I want to get out of here, to go home.

Q: And where is that?

A: Not in this armpit of the world, that's for sure. Okay, I'm from Vancouver, British Columbia.

Q: A Canadian then, are you?

A: Of course, I'm Canadian!

Q: Why are you so belligerent?

A: I didn't want to come here, but my wife insisted. And see where it got me?

Q: Where did it get you?

A: Thrown into jail, for heaven's sake. And God knows where my wife is.

Q: Your wife?

A: Hell, yes, you can't tell me it wasn't planned. She was in love with this...this "person" and he got me thrown into jail. Trumped-up charges, too.

Q: What charges?

A: They said I was carrying illegal drugs. Hell, I have this pre-scription. Xanax, supposed to cut down on my anxiety.

Q: And has it? Cut down on your anxiety?

A: Until I was thrown into this backwater jail in your backwater little country.

Q: Your wife talked you into coming here?

A: She likes to travel; I don't. But I figured, hell, I spend so much time at the office, I'd give in. Little did I know that she had ulterior motives.

Q: To meet this other man?

A: Yeah.

Q: How old are you?

A: Forty-eight. You think I'd know better, wouldn't you? But with the twins gone off to college...

Q: Twins?

A: A boy and a girl, Mark and Martha. Both at Simon Fraser. Oh, no, they didn't go far. That's still in Vancouver, but they are old enough to take care of themselves now, eh?

36

Q: How did your wife meet this man?
A: I'm an international lawyer, right? So I go to a lot of these functions.
Q: Functions?
A: Embassy parties. You know the sort of thing.
Q: And your wife met this man there?
A: Stands to reason, doesn't it? Oh, well, maybe it *was* my fault. Not paying attention, too wrapped up in work. Okay, I'm sorry about that. But it's done. Guess she got back at me all right though, didn't she?
Q: You mean leaving you for the other man.
A: And my being in jail. And so I'm stuck here, and I don't know what to do about it.
Q: An international attorney, you say, and you don't like to travel. And you're stuck in jail!
A: What can I say, guy?

As you see, a character and a situation is beginning to develop. You can infer all sorts of things about both. Most likely, what's already there will suggest a lot of other things — entanglements, settings, and characters.

This could be a serious play, but it also has elements of comedy — an international lawyer who doesn't like to travel, and then when he finally does, he ends up in jail.

If you like the character who has developed, you can go on with any number of scenes, starting with his being in jail or even starting well before that. Later we'll talk more about plot, but right away here you have any one of several things that could be the central problem or inciting incident — traveling, being thrown in jail, being jilted for another man. Or at best these are all complications, entanglements from which the man must try to free himself.

On the other hand, maybe you don't want to use your character further because he doesn't interest you, or you may use him but only as a secondary character, rather than as your protagonist. Don't eliminate any possibilities when you're first developing ideas for a play.

But since it takes only a few minutes to begin to develop a character, circumstances, setting and a plot, you may decide later that you don't like these characters or this idea at all. Then it's a simple matter of doing another interview, and another until you come up with ideas that you like.

This is somewhat different than doing straight improvisation, which is another technique for developing a play. In the character interview the person asking questions should stay as neutral as possible, so that the other character develops.

You can, however, do various types of improvisation with yourself playing the different roles or with someone else. In the situation that emerged in the interview, you may want to go on, making the interviewer a guard or an army officer who questions the prisoner. Then you have two characters beginning to emerge.

When you start to develop a play in this manner, your first character suggests other characters who then may be a part of the play. For example, two other logical characters are the wife and her lover or boyfriend. You may even have a scene with the twins where perhaps they show up to try to have their father released from prison.

Or maybe the wife hasn't really left the man for someone else. Maybe he just thinks she has. Why? Maybe she's trying to protect him in some way; maybe she's a spy who is just playing along with the other man to gain state secrets.

If you decide you do like what has occurred so far, you can go on adding scenes and situations.

Sometimes, however, a character simply will not emerge, or else the person is uninteresting or too far outside your realm of experience. Maybe you feel you don't know enough about international intrigue or politics to develop anything credible. You also would have a lot of work to do in establishing a frame of reference, a country in which this takes place. You would have to decide whether or not this is a democratic nation, whether the police are fair-minded people or bullies, and so on.

A variation of the character interview is to take two separate characters developed in this way and put them together. Again, I started here with no preconceived notions.

Q. **Who are you?**
A: **My name is Matilda. Matilda Crothers.**
Q: **How old are you, Matilda?**

A: Not that it's any of your damn business, but I'm sixty-two years old.

Q: Are you married?

A: Till my ever-lovin' hubby ran off with that floozie.

Q: You're divorced then.

A: Divorced! You've got to be kidding. I ain't paying no attorney money just to get rid of a man. I'm rid of him already.

Q: Then you're still married.

A: Not in my mind, I ain't. I ain't never gonna have nothin' to do with no men the rest of my life. Know what I mean?

Q: Sounds like you're pretty bitter.

A: Bitter ain't the word. There ain't no word that's strong enough. Him sticking me with all them debts, absconding with anything of value. A real — Nope, won't say the word in polite company.

Q: You're concerned about politeness then, courtesy?

A: That's the way Mama raised me. Isn't that the way your mama raised you?

Now you might put your two characters together in a particular setting. Where would be a logical place? Well, suppose it's in a courtroom where the man is being tried on charges of carrying drugs, the woman on another charge. We know her name is Matilda, but we don't know his yet. So we'll assign him the first name that comes to mind, George.

GEORGE: So they got you too, huh?

MATILDA: You talking to me?

GEORGE: Yeah, I'm talking to you. You don't see anyone else around, do you?

MATILDA: You're pathetic, you know? All men are pathetic.

GEORGE: Christ, try to start a conversation! What's your problem, sister?

MATILDA: I might ask you the same.

GEORGE: Okay, I'll tell you. We're visiting this little jerkwater country, see, and my wife gets me arrested and goes off with a damn gigolo or something.

MATILDA: Gigolo?

GEORGE: Another guy, whatever.

39

MATILDA: Your wife run off with someone else.

GEORGE: Yeah, so what?

MATILDA: People, huh? What can I tell you? My husband run off with this neighbor of ours. Thirty years younger than him, can you figure it?

GEORGE: So what did you do?

MATILDA: Nothing. Figured good riddance.

GEORGE: Sounds like you're pretty upset.

MATILDA: You mean you aren't?

GEORGE: Oh, yeah, I'm mad as hell. If I ever found them, I'd kill the —

MATILDA: Don't know where they went, huh?

GEORGE: Nah. You?

MATILDA: Not a clue. I always tried to tell myself I didn't care, but ... Don't know why I'm telling you all this.

GEORGE: You know, I do have some connections here. I know some people.

MATILDA: People?

Well, you see what can happen when you take what you know about two people. Maybe this scene would go nowhere, or maybe it could show the beginning of a relationship. Or maybe even if it does provide background information, you won't necessarily want to use it in the finished play. Maybe it's mostly exposition that can be brought out in other scenes where there is more direct conflict or tension, and you won't use a scene like this one at all.

At any rate, since the woman, in her interview, came across speaking a fairly low-class type of English, it's safe to assume that English is her native language. Is this the language of the country? If so, would her slang terms and manner of speech be so similar to the way English is sometimes spoken in North America?

Well, maybe she married her husband and came here with him. Maybe she made such a fuss about the country that he couldn't take it anymore and left. Or maybe what she says is basically true. You can go many, many different directions with what you have.

When George and Matilda talk together, however, keep consistent the glimmerings of characterization that developed in the character interview. For instance, both of them have a chip on their shoulders; both are somewhat sarcastic. Even their situations are similar, though their reactions are at least on the surface somewhat different.

BEGINNING WITH A TRAIT

Another way to begin to develop a character and then a situation or scene is to think of a specific personality trait. It can be anything. Suppose you choose "loving."

Remember that a play (or at least the usual kind of play) has to have conflict or there is no story. How then might you use this trait as the basis of a scene? All right suppose your character is a woman, all you really have decided about her so far. Now to show what a loving person she is, you need another character. Let's say it's her husband.

That's fine; in fact, it sounds like an excellent situation, a loving wife and a husband. But once again remember that there has to be conflict in a play. How could this possibly cause conflict? Well, suppose her husband is not very loving, at least on the surface. That is, he is not demonstrative, does not need constant reassurance of the way others feel about him.

Put the two of them in a scene together and see what happens, remembering that as yet you essentially know nothing about either. As you did with the character interview, simply let the scene flow. Let's say the characters are named Mary and Thom.

MARY: I love you, Thom. You're more important to me than anything else. Anything in the world.
THOM: Jesus, I wish you'd stop saying that.
MARY: What!?
THOM: It's like I'm penned in. Like I can't breathe.
MARY: How can I not say I love you?
THOM: I love you too, I guess.
MARY: You guess!
THOM: Damn it! I don't want to hurt you. I know how you feel. It's apparent as all get out how you feel. But you gotta understand. It's as if I can't breathe. As if —
MARY: Isn't love what marriage is all about? I love you, Thom. I always have. From the first time I saw you walk up on that porch with Donna and Frank—

41

THOM: See what I mean?

MARY: What?

THOM: Okay, I have it good. The best wife in the world. Hell, when I hear the other guys talk — I'm lucky. Luckier than I deserve. *(Pause)* I don't feel like I'm a person, Mary. A separate, breathing organism. I'm part of you, and you're part of me. And somehow we're this all-consuming ... damned thing.

MARY: I don't believe this. I mean I really don't believe it.

THOM: I'd give anything ... No. Almost anything, not to hurt you. Oh, man, this isn't the way I wanted it to be.

MARY: You wanted it to be? You mean you were planning —

THOM: How could I expect you'd understand! We're different, you and I. Maybe ... maybe not even reconcilable.

MARY: What ... what does that mean?

THOM: I'm going to leave, at least for awhile. I've made arrangements.

MARY: Jesus God!

THOM: Maybe not a divorce. I don't know. At this point I just don't know.

Again, I developed this on the spur of the moment, and did just a little editing.

The point is, you can take any trait and then figure out a situation and other characters in which to show this trait. Here you might have the beginning of a play, or maybe simply background information. Maybe the play begins where Mary is alone. Maybe she's suicidal; maybe she's bitter. Maybe she decides to seek revenge. There are countless ways in which you can use this as a point of departure.

PHYSICAL AND PERSONALITY TRAITS

A similar way to begin to develop a character and perhaps a set of conditions or circumstances is through word association. Start with one trait and then, on the basis of this first one, try to come up with a number of others—either personality or physical traits. Then take four or five of these and tie them together in a character sketch, a monolog or even a scene in which there is dialog.

As was the case with the preceding exercises, do not plan anything out ahead of time. But do keep in mind that the traits you finally choose have to be consistent with one another. For example, suppose you think of rumpled. A rumpled person may be a comfortable type person, kind-hearted, in other words. Go on saying the next trait that comes into your mind.

a. rumpled

b. kind-hearted

c. overweight

d. a workaholic

e. deliberate

f. worrier

g. devoted family man.

Where did the word "rumpled" come from? It simply popped into my mind. What does this mean? Well, perhaps the character's clothes don't fit well. Immediately, I guess, I thought of kind-hearted because a "rumpled" appearance suggests that the person cares about others more than about appearances.

If he doesn't care about appearances, maybe he also is overweight. But mainly he's overweight because he works too hard and doesn't exercise.

Usually, when I do this, I do not stop to analyze why one trait reminds me of another, but I did here to show you that the mind most often wants to make sense of things. So often what you come up with does fit with the preceding. If it doesn't, don't use it. That's why I suggest using only four or five out of several traits. Keep going with the list till you feel you have enough to choose from.

Now use the four or five you chose as a foundation on which to build character and a situation. Let's take the traits listed above, cutting out overweight and deliberate, and just let the ideas flow. This time, we'll do a monolog or soliloquy.

God, you know, no matter what I do, I look like I've slept all night in my clothes. That used to bother me, bother me like hell. I'd buy good clothes, clothes that would look great on anyone

43

else. A half hour later they'd look like I dug them out of the bottom of a laundry basket.

Don't get me wrong. If that were the biggest problem I have, I'd count myself lucky. I mean despite what people think of me, judging by appearances, I feel I'm a pretty good guy. Sure, I work too much. I know that, but doesn't everyone? Maybe not everyone, but you understand what I mean.

I came from the ghetto, you know? The worst section of Newark, New Jersey, and I had to get out all by myself. Could never let loose of my own bootstraps. Still think I shouldn't let go.

Sure, I know that's wrong, but I can't help it. I love my family, damn it, but I'm afraid everything is going to fall apart. I can't get over the fear. My job, my financial security.

So what happens? My family! I love my family. Wife and two daughters, ten and twelve now. Love them more than my own life. I mean I'd gladly die for them. And I want to spend more time with them. I do. I know the kids are growing up.

Wow, seems just yesterday Betsy was changing their diapers.

That's the trouble. Betsy was doing it. I was either out on the road working my butt off — that's before they promoted me to an office job — or I was too tired to ... Everything's passing me by. What am I going to do? I'm serious. What the hell am I going to do? It's like I'm two different people, opposites. One the worrier, the workaholic. The other the guy who cares about nothing so much as Betsy and the girls.

WORD ASSOCIATION

There are many other ways to try to come up with ideas. One also involves word association but now say any word that comes to mind, not just traits. For instance:

44

bad

dog

bite

dirty

slobber

neighbor

Damn it, I hate this. I can't even walk outside without that dog jumping all over me, wet paws, slobbering.

Hell, Jess and Guy have to know there's a city ordinance against this.

At least he doesn't bite, not like that silly little Pomeranian Ruth used to have.

I hate the whole situation, what with Jess being ill and all. Dying. If it were me, I'd just let things go. But what about everyone else? Old Mrs. Rockwell, scared half to death by the dog.

If they'd just tie him up. Sure, Guy says it's Jess. Can't stand the thought of anything penned up. What with Jess having so little time left, feeling penned in himself. "If I look outside and see Sam running loose, it's like I'm out there running too." That's what Guy told me he said.

Yeah, I talked to Guy, tried to get him to tie up the dog or keep him inside. I see his point of view, I really do, but the dog's going to hurt someone one of these times.

Be just another thing for everyone to complain about then.

"Bad enough those two queers moved in up the street," Bob Rockwell said "and then they let the damn dog loose."

I feel sorry for Jess and Guy. And I don't want anyone causing them trouble. But they've got to keep the dog penned up. They've just got to.

USING RANDOM WORDS

Pick three or four words at random, nouns or adjectives which at first glance have nothing in common. Then let your mind try to tie them together, to make sense out of them. Let's take: *bird* and *railroad* and *soup*. Do the same thing you did with the word association.

MARTHA: Ralphie was down by the railroad track the other day and you'll never guess what he saw.

RHONDA: Well, are you going to tell me or not?

MARTHA: This old hobo was eating soup out of a battered old pan.

RHONDA: So what?

MARTHA: Well, Ralphie said he saw all these feathers lying about.

RHONDA: Feathers? You mean he stole a chicken or something?

MARTHA: Naw, like they was feathers from a sparrow or some other little bird.

RHONDA: What are you trying to tell me, Martha?

MARTHA: I'm not trying to tell you anything. Just saying what Ralphie saw down by the railroad track.

RHONDA: You're saying something, all right. You're implying that this bum caught some little bird somehow and used it to make soup.

MARTHA: I'm not implying anything of the sort. You're inferring something out of something I said, that's all. And you darn well know it.

RHONDA: Homeless people are going to be taking over before long, you mark my words.

MARTHA: My Ralphie says it's the government's fault.

RHONDA: Government? It isn't anybody's fault except those men who are too damn lazy to try to make a decent living. They gotta go begging or stealing.

MARTHA: It wasn't a chicken, Rhonda, we settled that. It was a little, bitty bird. And he sure as heck didn't steal anything like that.

RHONDA: Can you imagine the diseases a bird like that might be carrying? I hear tell of folks dying of things like parrot fever.

MARTHA: Parrot fever! My God, Rhonda, it was a little bitty sparrow.

46

Sometimes, you can work with another person, simply beginning with a line one of you comes up with. One of you says it, and the other reacts. Go on from there without worrying about or trying consciously to go in any particular direction.

OBSERVATION AND MEMORY

So far, the exercises suggest ways of developing ideas for plays completely out of your own imagination. There are many other ways as well, with roots in reality. The sort of thing I mean begins with an observation or a memory.

Here's an exercise based on observing someone. Simply watch any person you see showing an emotion or performing an action. Then logically extend this in your mind. For instance, you see a woman hurrying along the sidewalk, in her mid- to late fifties. She has an anguished look on her face.

You start asking yourself questions about why she appears anguished. Maybe she's just heard that her daughter has been in a serious traffic accident and has been rushed to the hospital. The daughter is divorced with a mentally retarded son. He's home alone, and the woman, who has no car, is rushing to her daughter's house.

The woman, however, suspects that the boy is not as retarded as he appears. This is now her chance to prove her theory.

There you have an opening situation, a beginning scene, where the woman arrives and confronts the boy, a teenager about fifteen years old. The play is about their learning to accept each other on equal terms.

Or you see a man standing on a street corner constantly looking at his watch. Why is he looking at his watch? Obviously, he's expecting someone to pick him up. Who is it?

It's his friend. Why is the friend picking him up? Well, they've figured out the perfect plan for robbing the local bank — mostly to prove their intellectual superiority. Now the man is doubting that his friend is intellectually superior, else why would he be so damned late?

You can take any character or situation and play the "what if" game or ask questions about motives and circumstances. Don't edit yourself. Simply let the ideas flow without censoring them. Say the first thing that comes into your mind.

If you find a particular incident doesn't work, so what? You've wasted fifteen or twenty seconds, and maybe you've even learned which sorts of questions work well with this sort of exercise and which don't.

Or try remembering either something or someone from long ago. This is similar to the exercise mentioned in Chapter 2, where you try to recall everything you can about a person, a place or an event. Now instead of ending the exercise there, go on asking "what if" questions. I did this with a novel I recently finished.

When I was a kid, I joined a Boy Scout troop several miles away from home. I didn't know any of the other kids, except a cousin. Then I met the scoutmaster whom I came to like very much. He was disabled; he'd lost a leg in an accident at a strip mine.

I started thinking about him one day as a possible character. I don't know the circumstances of his accident; I'm not sure if I once knew or not. I'm sure I never knew what work he'd done.

So I started to ask "what if" questions. I developed a character who had been a policeman in Johnstown, Pennsylvania, not far from where I grew up. A bank robber lured him to a strip mine and set off dynamite, badly injuring Sam's leg. In my story, the leg is not amputated; instead, it's very thin. What does Sam do now that he's forced into retirement? He becomes a scoutmaster. There is a kidnapping, and the father of the boy who's kidnapped asks Sam to look for him. Thus begins Sam's career as a private eye. I hope to make him a continuing character in a series of detective novels.

BEGINNING WITH AN OBJECT

You can use an object as the basis of a play. For instance, recently, clearing out my aunt's house after her death, I came across an old baseball bat that apparently had belonged to my uncle. Much older than my aunt, he had grown up during the early part of the century.

I wondered why he had kept this baseball bat all these years. I knew he'd always been a staunch baseball fan, listening to every Pirates game on the radio or watching it on TV.

I started to speculate, to ask questions. Why was this particular bat (which I brought home from Pittsburgh to San Diego) so important to my uncle?

I picked it up, tested its weight and balance, and imagined myself swinging it as my uncle must have.

Then I started to think of things I know about him, and I built from there:

Despite the fact that his mother was a teacher, Bill quit high school. Here is where I start to speculate, to ask what *might* have happened.

Why did Bill quit school? Maybe a major league scout saw him play once and told him that in a few more years, when he matured physically, there'd be no stopping him. Okay, what position did he play? Pitcher, the glamor position.

Anyway, he couldn't wait for his dream to come true to play pro ball. He quit school to try out for the Pirates but didn't make it. As the scout had done, they told him: "Wait a few years, kid, and then come back and try again."

Disappointed, he joined the Army and went off to fight in World War I.

He didn't dislike the Army; he viewed it just as a way of marking time till his real life began. He kept playing pick-up baseball whenever he got the chance. Then disaster struck:

BILL: God, Celie, it was the worst thing that had ever happened to me. Can you imagine? There I was, lying in this damn trench outside Koblentz, waiting for the rain to stop, hoping the Jerries wouldn't discover us. All at once there's this terrible explosion, light so bright it blinded me for an instant. I look over and see my best buddy Frankie ... Jesus, there was nothing left of him. Not enough left even to know he'd once been a man, but not just any man. My best friend, maybe the only real friend I'd ever had.

We'd hit it off right away. We had so much in common, both coming from Western P.A. Two peas in a pod, except for my one burning passion, baseball. At that time, Celie, the only two things I cared about were baseball and Frank. In that order, God help me. Ah, hell, of course, I cared about my mom and my pop. But it was like they existed in another world. A world I sometimes thought wasn't real. Yet I knew it was real because that world was the Pittsburgh Pirates and the Brooklyn Dodgers. It was Honus Wagner and Tinker and Chance. Oh, Jesus, Celie, it wasn't till then that I noticed my arm. My pitching arm, goddamnit, cut to hell, covered with blood, like a piece of hacked up meat.

Oh, yeah, they saved it. The medics got the bleeding stopped, and they sent me to London. The whole damn way to London. Doctors and nurses did their damned best. But I'd never be a pitcher. Oh, God! People said I'd never be a pitcher. Can you understand what that felt like? Goddamn. All I could think about was that arm. What the hell kind of person was I anyhow, thinking only of that arm? Not of Frank or the girl he was going to marry, or his mom and dad back in Wilkensburg.

Funny, isn't it, that he came from there. Not that far away, you know. Twenty, twenty-five miles? Something like that. And yet we meet on the other side of the world.

God, I was selfish. But I had such dreams. Such dreams, Celie. I've let it affect my whole damned life, don't you see?

You can begin with a photo or a painting or a document. One of the things I have framed and hanging on my dining room wall is my great, great uncle Nicholas Stevens' discharge papers from the Civil War. Not the original papers, but rather a "fancied up" version with color pictures of land and sea battles, soldiers on horseback, flags and drums.

At the bottom of the document, it says this was prepared for my great-great uncle by the war records office and presented to his wife in 1904.

I take the very sketchy information I know about my grandmother's uncle and speculate about him. Why did he wait so long to have this paper prepared? Well, he probably married later in life because I know he and his sister Kate, both unmarried, reared my grandmother whose own mother, Arabella Clark Eichelberger, had died in childbirth. Grandma's father had remarried, having a second set of kids with his new wife, letting my grandma and my great-uncle Marsh stay with relatives. I don't even know if Nick and Kate were his own relatives or Arabella's.

From here on this is all speculation, as again I pose questions, based on what I know. Why did Uncle Nick wait so long to marry? Well, he hadn't yet found anyone he was crazy about marrying. Then fifteen or so years after the war, Uncle Marsh and then Grandma were born. It was the 1880s. When Nick and Kate came to the funeral, my great-grandfather — his name was Eli Eichelberger — gave his two children to Kate and Nick to rear. Did Nick resent this? No, he was a kind man who loved kids. What sort of work did he do? He was a blacksmith in Hopewell, Pennsylvania, where they lived.

Why did Kate never marry? Maybe she was once spurned by a young man she deeply loved.

What did people think in that time and place of a brother and sister living together and rearing two kids? There was gossip. Some even said it was a matter of incest, that Grandma and Uncle Marsh were Nick and Kate's kids.

How did this affect my grandmother and her brother, Kate and Nicholas? Having a sort of warped sense of humor, Nick and Kate decided to let people go on thinking what they wanted. Uncle Nick had been a hero in the battle of Fort Sumpter so, for this reason, people respected him and left him pretty much alone, except to visit his smithy to have their horses shod.

Then a new preacher moved to town, heard the gossip and decided to do something to end this dreadful abomination of a family arrangement.

So even though it took a circuitous route to get to this point, we have a central problem, a conflict. This might be where the play begins; the rest is brought out in the exposition.

The play is about how the preacher's condemnation affects the community. How do people react? What do they do? How does it then affect Kate and Nick, Grandma and Uncle Marsh?

The play begins in the midst of the conflict. It ends in 1904 with a scene where my grandmother and her brother arrange to have this wonderful document prepared and framed and presented to Nick, who married once Grandma and Great-Uncle Marsh were old enough to get along pretty well by themselves.

So there's a beginning and an ending; as a playwright, I have to proceed logically from one point to the other.

UNRELATED ACTIONS

You can experiment with other ways of developing ideas. For instance, take two seemingly unrelated actions and figure out how they might be tied together logically:

a. a woman screaming on the bank of a river for someone to save her baby who is being swept away by the current.

b. a man's escape from jail.

Now come up with a plot to tie these two things together, or develop some sort of relationship between the man and woman, taking into account these two important events in their lives.

a. The man comes along and saves the baby. The woman is grateful and agrees to hide him from the authorities. He becomes abusive, and so on.

b. The man feels the woman will draw attention to him, so he knocks her out and kidnaps her. The baby drowns, and the woman is a prisoner. She will do anything to get revenge.

Of course, there could be many other scenarios too.

Do keep in mind that it is the important events of a life, not the mundane events, that test people's mettle, that bring out the unexpected, that make them characters worthy of an audience's attention.

STREAM OF CONSCIOUSNESS

Sometimes it works simply to do stream of consciousness writing or audio taping. Simply say anything that comes into your head without trying to censor it. For instance:

One day I was sitting at my desk when I looked out the window and saw a cow wandering up the street. A cow? I thought. What would a cow be doing in the North Park section of San Diego? Oh, well, it didn't matter, I thought, so I went back to work, typing a report for the interplanetary council on the effects of oxygen on the growth of Martian fungi.

A cow? My thoughts kept returning to the odd spectacle. I had to find out what was going on. I stepped outside into the street where the stench nearly drove me mad. Stench? What from?

I saw this woman nearly ready to pass out from the smell. As a matter of fact, I caught her in my arms just as she started to fall. A man holding a knife ran up. "What are you doing with my wife?" he asked.

"Your wife? I'm just trying to keep her from passing out."

The woman opened here eyes. "My God, is it really you, Sean?" she asked the man.

"It's me. I've been looking for you all over town. I'd heard you had escaped and were being brought here."

"Escaped," I said. "From what?"

"The terrorists who would kill us."

"What Sean means," the woman said, "is that he and I ... well, we're the ones who led the revolt."

"What revolt?" I asked.

I wrote the above with no thought at all in mind where it might lead. And already several possibilities are suggested. The man with the knife and the woman who says she's his wife are dangerous criminals who now capture the protagonist. Throughout the next few scenes, they try to convince him that he should believe in their cause (whatever it is; I haven't yet thought that far ahead). He resists; they try threats, cajoling, appeals to his sense of humanity.

The play then is about learning to trust, to believe, and about whether the trust is well-founded or not. I'd totally disregard the first part about the cow, the report on fungi, etc. It was just a device to get me started. So the play itself actually might begin back at my (the man's) apartment. Let's say his name is Richard, and that the woman's name is Tasha.

SEAN: Hey, man, you know, everyone's got to believe in something. I found that out the hard way.

TASHA: What Sean means is that unless you fight for what you believe, some day you're going to find all your freedoms gone. Kaput. You know?

RICHARD: So you expect me to go along with whatever mad scheme it is you're trying to —

SEAN: You're one of the elite, man, one of the untouchables.

RICHARD: *(astounded)* What the hell —

TASHA: Have you ever seen anyone killed? I mean murdered, assassinated. A parent? A child? Right in front of your eyes.

RICHARD: No, and I doubt that you have eith —

SEAN: Look, creep — Ah, hell, you don't understand.

RICHARD: You're right; I don't. So why don't you try explaining?

You may find the scene suggests characters and a plot, or maybe it doesn't. If not, try again. You don't have much invested.

GIVEN CIRCUMSTANCES

Another trick is to begin with given circumstances, things you decide at random. For example, two friends meet in the park. It is late at night. One is terribly frightened; the other is simply angry.

What you need to do is figure out the reasons why both characters are there. What are their intentions, their goals? What has motivated them? Why is the one frightened, the other angry?

Maybe they're teenagers, a girl and a boy. The girl has asked the boy to meet him because of a fight she had with her father. The boy, her best friend, knows she has a terrible temper and is angry at once again being sucked into her battles with her father. Yet he is afraid to leave her in the park unprotected. From here, the scene can go in a lot of different directions. It can be about a dysfunctional family; about the aftermath of a gang's attack on the two characters or whatever.

Or: The location is a street corner of a busy intersection in the downtown section of a big city. A man is leaning against a doorway, while another man is tugging on his arm to get him to move. Here are a couple of suggestions for how the scene might progress.

    a. The first man is resisting being taken at gunpoint to an automatic teller machine where the other man will rob and most likely kill him.

    b. The man leaning against the doorway is overcome with grief and plans to kill himself. His friend is trying to talk him out of it.

Certainly these are just isolated scenes, but they easily could become part of a longer piece once you figure out where they fit in and what they have to do with the major events of the play.

Of course, if I were going to go on with any of these ideas, I'd think them through much more carefully, refine them, use them only as a starting point in outlining a play. In the next couple of chapters, we'll explore more about what this means, more about the parts of a play and what has to go into one to make it workable, producible.

Many plays are developed through improvisation. One such play developed at a summer stock theatre where I was an actor. We started only with the idea that the play would take place in Appalachia, and each of the participants — the actors from the theatre — would develop a character. Then we would get together with one or more of the other characters and talk about things that concerned us.

It developed that the play then became about a woman who'd left the area after a fight with her father. Over the years she'd become a successful and well-respected television journalist. Now she's returning home. There were many in the town who condemned her for betraying her roots, for becoming "uppity." And so begins the conflict, the woman versus her father and most of the rest of the town. To complicate matters, the woman's mother had died shortly after she left, and she hadn't returned for the funeral.

ACTIVITIES

Try any of the following, either by yourself or, if you are in a class, with fellow students to see if any suggest a plot or characters or conflict which interests you.

Trust your instincts. There's no good or bad way of doing them, and your ideas will be as good as anyone else's. It's what you later do with the idea that counts.

1. Either with someone else or by playing both roles yourself, develop a character through the interview method. Of course, if you are using this book as part of a class, one person can choose to be "it," with the others asking questions at random.

2. Develop a second character through the interview method. Then put this character and the one from Activity #1 together and have them talk to each other. You can include whatever you wish that has developed so far, and you also can add new traits.

3. Choose one of the following character traits, and think of a person who might have such a trait. To portray it, have the character talk with someone else who would logically be a partner, just as the husband was in the example from this chapter. Have the two characters oppose each other in some way as a result of the trait.

a. moralistic

b. unscrupulous

c. a whiner

d. a bully

e. dependent

f. forceful

g. anti-social

Now do the same thing with traits you name.

4. Develop character traits through word association. You can do this by yourself or by having members of the class list traits in turn. Come up with no more than eight or ten and then use four or five of them to develop a character. You can have the character deliver a monolog, or you can place the person in a

56

scene with someone else. Remember that at the basis of a good scene is conflict, and conflict also is a good way to make a monolog interesting to an audience.

5. Now do exactly the same thing, using word association, but not limiting yourself to character or physical traits. Again, write either a monolog or a scene with another character. Be sure to include conflict.

6. Choose one of the following lists and tie the words or terms together in a scene or monolog.

   a. car, bestseller, lamp

   b. statue, file cabinet, ceiling

   c. Broadway show, applesauce, assault rifle

   d. clock, paperweight, mountain stream

   e. biographer, clump of earth, dishpan

Now try the same thing with your own random set of words. Or if you are part of a class, write three separate words or terms on three separate pieces of paper. Have someone collect these, and then have each person draw three slips of paper. Of course, if you have two words that are the same, put one back and draw another.

7. Observe someone out in public — in a restaurant, a line at the post office or bank, at a grocery store, etc. What emotions do you think you can read on their faces or in their body language? Write a scene or monolog explaining why the person is feeling this way.

8. Think of someone from your past, someone who made a big impression. Take what you know about the person and then ask "what if" questions about parts of the person's life that you don't know. Build a scene or a monolog around this.

9. Take an object from your room or home and build a scene around it, as I did with my uncle's baseball bat. Do the same thing with a totally unfamiliar object, one that you see in a second-hand store or in someone else's home.

10. Use a document, a painting, or a photo as the basis of a scene you build using the "what if" technique.

11. Take two unrelated activities, and incorporate them into a

scene. Choose both from among the following, or come up with ideas of your own. Or trade papers with someone else in a class.

    a. a woman running down the street singing at the top of her lungs.

    b. a teenager trying to open a car door.

    c. a man walking swiftly through a hallway, glancing back over his shoulder.

    d. a person getting hit by a bicycle on a busy sidewalk.

    e. a man or woman stumbling and falling in a coffee shop.

    f. someone holding a butcher knife and running after another person.

12. Try some stream of consciousness writing or audio taping, saying anything that comes into your head. Write at least four or five paragraphs or do thirty seconds to a minute of tape. Now go back over this and see what ideas you can extract that might be the basis for a scene. Write the scene.

13. Take the following given circumstances, and develop reasons or motivations for the characters. Then come up with your own given circumstances, or write them out and trade papers with someone else.

    a. It is late at night. A man is sitting on the curb. A woman is standing nearby biting her lip.

    b. The setting is a department store. Two teenagers, a boy and a girl, are arguing.

    c. It is seconds before the playoff game. On the sidelines, two men rush toward each other.

    d. It is just before quitting time at the office. The boss hurries up to the assistant's desk.

    e. It is lunchtime. A man and a woman enter a restaurant by separate doors. They immediately leave together.

    f. Two people stand in the middle of a deserted cornfield late at night. They are both obviously very tired.

CHAPTER 4

Beginning a Script

If you have not done a lot of writing, it can be a daunting experience to be told you have to write an entire play.

My advice then is not to think in terms of writing a whole play. Think of it as writing bits and pieces — characters, monologs, scenes, encounters.

In past chapters, you've seen already that there are many ways to start. You can begin by developing characters you then put together in a particular situation or scene. Maybe they're just exploring interests, ideas, backgrounds to help you yourself clarify the sort of people they are and what has gone before in their lives that will affect future actions.

A scene in a play does need direction, but that can come later. At first, you may want only to think about the elements that will make up the play. It has been said, for instance, that the more a playwright knows about his characters, the more convincing they will be. This doesn't mean that everything that the writer knows must be transferred to the final script. Much is by implication. For instance, the scene from Chapter 3 where the man and woman meet in the courtroom may not be compelling enough to include in a final play, unless it were trimmed way down and used only as a starting point.

GIVING THE SCRIPT DIRECTION

Theatre and plays have more direction at all times than life seems to much of the time. While we often deal with important issues, much of life seems aimless. But plays deal with important concepts and issues that are always at the forefront. The playwright explores them and makes statements about them that are brought out in encounters and problems that are important to the characters.

The scenes so far have been designed only to get you started writing and thinking as a playwright. If you wish, you can develop some of them further. But you also can start with something new. At this point, however, you need to be thinking seriously about characters and ideas you want to continue to work with as you write a complete play, one-act or a full-length.

You can begin with either one. Some people find it less daunting to begin with the one-act because it is shorter. On the other hand, your idea may be too large to be contained within the shorter form. Probably at this point you aren't sure yet which form your ideas fit. That's fine; as you go along it will in all likelihood become clearer to you.

Generally, it is easier to begin with a one-act since the idea usually isn't as encompassing as that for a longer play. On the other hand, Synge's *Riders to the Sea*, sometimes called the perfect one-act, is highly condensed in its tale of tragedy connected with drownings and the sea. A play like this certainly would require as much work as one that is full length.

How will the ideas come clear to you? It comes back to the same question we've been asking over the first few chapters: How and where do you begin?

If you don't already have an idea for a play, use one or more of the techniques for getting ideas that were suggested in Chapters 1 and 3. But do think now in terms of continuing to work with these ideas. As you continue to write more plays, you'll probably discover that you'll begin in various ways.

Later you will learn more about developing the elements of plot, dialog and character. But for now, once you have the beginnings of an idea (or even if you don't), you might begin writing a monolog or several monologs, in which your characters state what is most important in their lives, what has affected them to make them the sort of people they are.

UNIVERSALITY

When you do monologs such as these, make sure they touch on reasons and incidents that shaped the character. This is the sort of thing Bill says in his monolog about baseball or that Sarah says in her audition. Sarah's is more focused, but it certainly took longer to sharpen and hone than Bill's, which at best will become a short segment of a play. *The Monologue*, on the other hand, is meant to be complete in itself, or at least complete as one section of a larger performance piece, just as a one-act play is only one of the pieces in an evening of one-acts.

What sorts of problems or concerns can you deal with? Certainly, they should have universality, which means they are relevant to an audience. Universality actually means a character or plot or play has meaning for everyone. Of course, that's the ideal. It's probably better to think in terms of the play's having meaning for most people whom you want to see it, the audience you envision for it.

Universality, of course, can take many forms. We can relate to feeling trapped as Tom does in *The Glass Menagerie* and to the evils of apartheid as expressed in Fugard's *Master Harold and the Boys*, even though we are unlikely to find ourselves enmeshed in the central characters' situations in either play. Although we may not be Mormons and many of us are not gay, we can relate to the pressures the central character feels in Tony Kushner's *Angels in America*.

Yet everyone can relate to a character's passions, the things that he or she may care about even too much. Often we have our own passions, our own strong causes, such as the need to eliminate prejudice based on color, ethnicity, religion or sexual orientation.

Even if we do not have our own strong passions, we all know people who are entirely obsessed — with being the world's best businessman, the perfect mate, the highest achiever. They chase their passions, their dreams to the ultimate.

Sometimes they gain what they want; at other times they do not. Sarah in *The Monologue* wants to "get past" the fact that she was sexually abused. Bill wants either to succeed as a pitcher despite his injury or maybe to find a substitute passion, something to which he can devote his life.

Will these two succeed or not? Sarah probably will not, though she may have a relatively happy life. Bill may work hard enough to overcome his injury, like Olympic runner Glenn Cunningham did when his legs were so badly scarred that he was told he would never walk again, let alone run. Plays deal with this sort of thing, things that truly matter to the characters and to their larger lives.

Sometimes the protagonist is successful in fulfilling a goal or a need. At other times, he or she is defeated. There are countless stories of people feeling utterly defeated when by most people's standards, their lives have been a success. A few years back a high school senior committed suicide because he'd failed to pin a wrestling opponent. Yet the young man was not a wrestler and had never tried wrestling before. And the person who pinned him was a state high school wrestling champ.

It didn't matter that the boy who killed himself had been a super achiever in a dozen other ways, that he was a straight A student, that he was a soloist in his high school choir, that he had the lead in plays, that he was named to both the all-state basketball and football teams for the past two or three years, that he enjoyed working with and helping to tutor young kids. He failed at something he'd never previously tried, and because of this could not forgive himself. And so one noon hour, when his parents were at work, he came home from school, took out his father's shotgun, loaded it, stuck the barrel into his mouth and pulled the trigger.

The playwright Tennessee Williams reportedly felt often that he was a failure, even though plays like *The Glass Menagerie* and *A Streetcar Named Desire* have assured him a place in theatrical history.

Plays have to be about strong feelings, strong passions, strong beliefs, about standing up for what you believe, about achieving, as Don Quixote called it in *Man of La Mancha*, "The Impossible Dream."

You do not have to begin developing a play around such a passion, but this should come as you go along. Even plays that are strictly for entertainment revolve around a central problem, or there would be no plot. You do have to deal with times of importance in the character's lives, if you want to write a play that is worthwhile.

In most of the examples I provided in the previous chapters, the idea eventually did come around to something that mattered. George and Matilda both are obsessed with their spouses running off with other people. Nicholas and Kate Stevens are faced with public condemnation. Mary is obsessed with loving Thom and with being the perfect wife. She is so obsessed with it, in fact, that she goes completely overboard and may have sounded the death knell for the relationship.

The "rumpled" character is so concerned with financial security (understandable in light of his background) that he, like Mary, probably is losing his family.

So again, where do you begin? With something important or something that has the potential to develop into something important. It does not have to be a character. As you learned, it can be an idea, a set of circumstances, a setting. But each of these has to be of importance to you as the writer, in some way, whether literally or as the symbol of something else, and to the characters.

What do I mean by saying they can be a symbol of something else? Bill's ruined chance at playing baseball could be a symbol of his failure throughout life; it could stand as the symbol for universal feelings of regret, for wishing things would be different, for the feeling many people have that their lives have been wasted, that they never did achieve what they set out to accomplish. They didn't find the cure for cancer, write the great American novel, become the most pious of individuals.

What can a writer then do with this sort of symbol?

ESTABLISHING CONFLICT

First, all characters — even those minor characters who are included mostly as devices to further the actions — have intentions or goals. It is when these intentions come into conflict in some way that we have a storyline. But reaching the goals has to be important; something vital has to be at stake. The conflict, the struggle has to constitute something utterly compelling in the lives of the characters, a prize, if you will, that is worth taking a lot of risks to gain.

In real life, most people would prefer to have things go smoothly, although we do hear of those who thrive on opposition and conflict. (I know a novelist, for instance, who doesn't appear to be happy unless he is baiting people in some way. For some reason, this man thrives on "manufactured" conflict and tension, but that is not the usual standard.) People want their lives to run smoothly; they want to achieve things without coming up against insurmountable or nearly insurmountable odds. Yet, if things are handed to us too easily, we tend not to value them.

63

A good example of this: My father gave private music lessons. At times, he felt sorry for kids who came from very poor families and offered to give them free lessons. This didn't work. Why? He heard a parent saying one day, after his son had missed the previous week's lesson, "It didn't matter whether he missed or not. After all, the lessons are free."

The things that mean the most to us usually are those that we work for. Yet most of us would rather not make enormous sacrifices, going without food or adequate clothing, for instance, to have money to take guitar or piano lessons. But in a play, where everything is running smoothly or at least without great difficulty from beginning to end, there is absolutely no way to keep an audience's attention. Perhaps the novelty of a situation will do it for a time, but not for an entire play.

A character has to want something and then must try to reach that goal. So far, the problems posed for Bill, for Nick and Kate, for George and so on, are only problems, introduced but unresolved. The characters' intentions to this point, or at least those the audience knows about, have been thwarted in some way. But the characters have not yet reacted to these problems. The reaction, more than the problem, is what is important because it shows the type of characters with which we are dealing. And character, whether the most important element or not, certainly is the one that makes most plays come alive.

How do the characters react when encountering an obstacle to reaching their goals? This is what provides the basis for an interesting play.

What will Mary do to rectify the situation? Obviously, it's intolerable. Will she try her best to mend whatever is wrong with her marriage? Will she change her definition of what it means to be a perfect wife? Or will her husband's revelation that he is fed up and is leaving make her react in another way? As stated earlier, perhaps she becomes so furious at him for not appreciating her that she decides to get even, maybe even to make him suffer or kill him. Then you have an entirely different play.

A character is determined to reach a certain goal. Maybe this has been the person's aim all along. But now there is conflict in reaching it, and so the character must modify behavior in some respect, most certainly must try even harder to achieve whatever he or she wants.

In this book, we will deal mostly with story plays, those that have a plot. There are other types of structures, which will be touched on in a later chapter. But even in these latter plays, there has to be some goal, some prize that keeps us interested. We have to identify with the two characters who are waiting for Godot to appear in Samuel Beckett's *Waiting for Godot,* even though we have no idea what they are waiting for, or why the character of Godot is supposed to appear to them.

In Chapter 5, which deals more completely with dramatic structure, you will learn more about building a plot. For now it is enough to keep in mind that there are certain basic elements that make up a play, and they contribute to the idea or story or the central character's striving toward a goal.

Even *The Monologue* has a basic plot of sorts. Will Sarah be able to overcome or put her problem of being abused into perspective well enough to continue to function fairly normally? The answer is yes, at least for the time being. It fact, it is her honesty and openness, no doubt, which help her get the role in the play.

Even in my own play, *One Moment in Time,* where there is no single plot, no one protagonist striving to overcome odds stacked against him or her, each set of characters will encompass a mini-story. The play will not be linear, proceeding from one point in time to a later point in time. Rather it will jump from one set of murderer/victims to another, examining many points in their past lives.

There will be conflict leading up to each murder. So, in effect, *One Moment in Time* will be made up of a series of loosely related situations, intentions and goals. However, each character will want something, which may change from the beginning of the play to the end. Yet it all can be stated in a single, simple sentence: Each character wants or seeks fulfillment, or a happy life, but each on his or her own terms and according to his or her own definition.

In writing this play, I'll include some monologs that sum up what the characters feel and what they want out of life. I'll have dialogs between the people who become murderers and those who become the victims. Since the play is nonconventional in plot, I'll probably just let my characters spend some time together talking:

MICHAEL: **What is this crap, man? I told you I'm damn sick of hamburgers every night.**
ED: **Oh, yeah, then why don't you do the cooking?**
MICHAEL: **Right, like I have the time to do that. Going to school, holding down a job, trying to find a little time to study.**
ED: **You think I got it easy?**
MICHAEL: **Easy? Damn right you do. You go to work, you come home, you sit in front of the TV —**
ED: **Don't I wish.**

Conflict! I don't know if I'll use such a scene as this, but I want to show the deteriorating relationship between Ed and Michael. Later I'll go back and write scenes from their earlier lives, both before and after they met. But at first I won't worry about fitting these things together or even whether I'll use all of them. I may not, but even if I don't, I'll learn a lot about my characters and their situations and conflicts simply by letting them talk to each other on paper.

INTENTIONS AND GOALS

The characters in a play have goals, which they try repeatedly to reach. If they did not try repeatedly, the goal would not seem worthwhile, just as the free music lessons didn't to the boy's parent.

Each time characters try to reach the prize, each time until perhaps the final conflict, they are defeated or at least suffer setbacks, so that they change their tactics somewhat and their manner of approach. If they were to win immediately, if they were to reach a goal the first time they expend any effort at it, the play would be a "so what?" sort of piece.

We learn most about a character; we sympathize most with a character who has to struggle to fulfill a goal. There's little else to hold our attention. Or maybe we don't either sympathize or empathize with the characters, but we stay with them hoping they'll get their comeuppance. Regina, the protagonist in Lillian Hellman's *The Little Foxes*, is anything but sympathetic. Yet we

66

want to know what happens to her. Here's a very scaled down account of the plot.

> The Hubbard family attempts to raise money to establish a cotton mill in a nearby town. At the opening of the play, Regina's husband Horace, president of the local bank, has been in the hospital, the result of a heart ailment. His wife Regina's letters to him fail to bring the money necessary for the Hubbards' venture. This is Regina's first attempt at reaching her goal. Second, she sends her daughter Alexandra to bring Horace back home.
>
> However, Horace refuses to provide the money Regina and her brothers need. In the meantime Regina's brother and a nephew steal securities belonging to Horace and cut Regina out of her share in the entrepreneurial venture. She learns this from Horace, who planned not to seek revenge, and she becomes enraged.
>
> The shock of realizing what his wife is really like causes Horace to have a heart attack. She could give him medication and save his life. Instead, Regina lets him die. Then she confronts her brothers with the theft and demands seventy-five percent of the profits not to expose them.
>
> She changes her tactics at various times and ends up making even more money than she imagined.

Sometimes, the intentions in each scene may differ and yet contribute to the overall goal. A physically handicapped woman tries to escape a burning house. She's paralyzed. Her first goal is to struggle into her wheelchair, which she cannot see because of the thick smoke in the room. Next, she has to get the bedroom door open, but the knob burns her hand. Then she has to get past a wall of flame in the hall and so on.

Each intention is different, but each contributes to the

overall goal of getting outside the burning house.

Of course, the conflict and struggle in most plays isn't that simple or direct. Rather it is because of the type of person someone is, because of background and expectations, that the character strongly needs to reach a certain goal.

In large part due to the type of personalities the characters have, they have different perceptions and expectations, and to a degree different backgrounds. (A college professor would have a much different background than a short order cook, though both have been used as protagonists in plays: Ionesco's *The Lesson*, for the former, and Terrence McNally's *Frankie and Johnny at the Clare de Lune*, for the latter, for instance.)

In figuring out intentions, you need to keep in mind that a character is both pushed by the past and pulled by the future. Thus, the person is set on a course that has to continue throughout the play. There is simply no stopping. Certainly, the person has some control of life, but what he or she is, as the result of genes, background and expectations, dictates how the person will handle life.

In Arthur Miller's *Death of A Salesman*, Willy Loman has had some success as a salesman but now his trips on the road are ending in failure. He wants to be a success so his boys will look up to him, so his wife will be provided for. He pleads for the chance to go on the road again. He fantasizes about what might have been. And in the end he kills himself so his family will have his life insurance.

His past made him desperate to be successful; this pushes him forward. At the same time, he is pulled toward the goal, tries however he can to be successful (which he defines in terms of finances) and finally finds a way, by killing himself and thus providing life insurance money for his wife and two sons. He is pushed by past failures and pulled toward his goal.

COMMUNICATION THROUGH IMPLICATION

Usually, in life we do not directly state what we want. Rather we imply or give clues. The same thing should hold true in a play. In the following monolog from Oscar Wilde's *The Importance of Being Earnest*, Gwendolen, in love with Jack, has just discovered that Cecily is his ward. Here is what she says:

GWENDOLEN: Oh! It is strange he never mentioned to me that he had a ward. How secretive of him! He grows more interesting hourly. I am not sure, however, that the news inspires me with feelings of unmixed delight. *(Rising and going to her)* I am very fond of you, Cecily: I have liked you ever since I met you! But I am bound to state that now that I know that you are Mr. Worthing's ward, I cannot help expressing a wish you were — well, just a little older than you seem to be — and not quite so alluring in appearance. In fact, if I may speak candidly —
CECILY: Pray do! I think that whenever one has anything unpleasant to say, one should always be quite candid.
GWENDOLEN: Well, to speak with perfect candor, Cecily, I wish that you were fully forty-two, and more than usually plain for your age. Ernest has a strong upright nature. He is the very soul of truth and honour. Disloyalty would be as impossible to him as deception. But even men of the noblest possible moral character are extremely susceptible to the influence of the physical charms of others. Modern, no less than ancient history, supplies us with many most painful examples of what I refer to. If it were not so, indeed, history would be quite unreadable.

Of course, what Gwendolen is saying is that she is terribly jealous of Cecily. But she says it only through implications.

Or look at the following scene from my play *NHI: No Human Involved* in which somebody is poisoning food left in city trash cans and thus killing street people who eat this food.

NADINE: A serial killer maybe.
JOE: There's no pattern, no ritual.
NADINE: Just because something usually happens doesn't mean it always will.
JOE: Yeah, well ...
NADINE: You're not convinced.
JOE: What about you? Any theories?
NADINE: You know I'm not supposed to have theories.
JOE: Is that bitterness I hear?
NADINE: I don't like this any more than you do. But you're

in a better position. You were on the force. You know
how to handle things. *(Pause)* I sympathize, Joe, and I'll
do whatever I can.
JOE: Short of jeopardizing your job.
NADINE: Hey, look, Joe, there are few women who even
make sergeant in this town. Let alone lieutenant.
JOE: And you wouldn't want to besmirch your spotless —
Sorry, you deserve better than that.
NADINE: I understand your frustration. And unofficially ...
damn it, Joe, I'll do what I can.

A lot more is being implied than actually stated. Joe, a former policeman and a man who was forced to live on the streets
himself after losing his job due to budget cuts, is having lunch
with a former colleague, a woman who has remained his friend.
Their conflict is about the fact that he wants her to help find the
person who is poisoning the food in city trash bins and Nadine's
fear of losing her job.

Yet neither comes right out and says what they mean. In
effect, they negotiate. At first, Nadine sympathizes but doesn't
want to do anything to help. Then comes the first offer at compromise. Apparently out of friendship, she decides that she'll do
what she can, so long as it doesn't jeopardize her job. Yet as part
of the negotiation, she implies that Joe has to understand that
once it does jeopardize her job, she can't give him any more help.

HOOKING THE VIEWER

Each play should start with a "hook," something that
immediately grabs the audience's attention. This is because contemporary audiences are so used to fast-paced entertainment
that they won't sit still while little or nothing is happening.

Most movie films begin with a scene that immediately
hooks the audience's attention; most TV plays begin with a teas-
er to hook the viewers so they'll be sure to stayed tuned during
the upcoming commercials.

No longer can we have plays that begin like the following
from Anna Cora Mowatt's nineteenth century play, *Fashion*. The
only purpose here is to provide exposition, background information about the central characters.

ZEKE: Dere's a coat to take de eyes ob all Broadway! Ah! Missy, it am de fixin's dat make de natural born gemman. A libery for ever! Dere's a pair ob insuppressibles to 'stonish de colored population.

MILLINETTE: *(Very politely)* Oh, oui, Monsieur Zeke. *(Aside)* I not comprend one word he say!

ZEKE: I tell 'ee what, Missy, I'm 'stordinary glad to find dis a bery 'spectabul like situation! Now, as you've made de acquaintance ob dis here family, and dere you've had a supernumerary advantage ob me — seeing dat I only receibed my appointment dis morning. What I wants to know is your publicated opinion, privately expressed, ob de domestic circle.

MILLINETTE: You mean vat *espèce* vat kind of personnes are Monsieur and Madame Tiffany? Ah! Monsieur is not de same ting as Madame, — not at all.

ZEKE: Well, I s'pose he ain't altogether.

MILLINETTE: Monsieur is man of business, — Madame is lady of fashion. Monsieur make de money, — Madame spend it. Monsieur nobody at all. — Madame everybody altogether. Ah! Monsieur Zeke, de money is all dat is *necessaire* in dis country to make one lady of fashion. Oh! it is quite anoder ting in la belle France!

An audience wants something that captures their attention immediately, whether by having unusual characters, a lot of action or a strange situation. Compare the opening of *Fashion* to those of the openings that follow. The first is from a play called *Scars*:

(As the lights come up, TIMOTHY is kneeling by one of the two single beds, hands clasped, resting on the mattress. He doesn't glance up as BOB enters, carrying two suitcases.)

TIMOTHY: *(Praying)* Our Thomas Wolfe, who art in heaven, hallowed be thy name. Thy novels be read; thy writing be loved in the rest of earth as it is in Carolina. *(Astounded, BOB stops for a moment and then crosses to the other bed. He turns, keeping an eye on TIMOTHY.)*

TIMOTHY: Give us this day our daily prose, and forgive us our writing blocks as we forgive your critics. *(BOB sets down his suitcases, shaking his head.)*

TIMOTHY: *(Rising and facing BOB, he grins.)* **There's no god. No heaven, except what we create in our minds. Thomas Wolfe is my god.** *(He holds out his hand.)* **I'm Timothy U. Landis.**

BOB: *(Taking his hand)* **Hi, Bob Thompson.**

TIMOTHY: **Since I arrived first, I took this side of the room, this bed, this half of the dresser.** *(He points to a large, squat chest of drawers.)*

BOB: **Fine, I have no preference.**

TIMOTHY: **Each one of us has preferences. We simply have to find what they are and not deny them. We have to be true to ourselves.**

Begin with a high point, something that is unusual or needs explaining. Why, for instance, does Timothy pray to Thomas Wolfe? What sort of person is he? Even though you do this, you can bring in a lot of exposition: Timothy and Bob will be roommates, Timothy arrived at the room first, and so on.

Begin with something out of the ordinary. The following is from a one-act play, *An Avalanche of Tenors*, by Louis Phillips, which is, to say the least, an unusual beginning.

We are in the lobby of a Cuckoo-Clock Inn somewhere on the fringes of the Alps. For sake of argument, let us say we are in Durrance Valley, where the altitude is below 300 meters or 1,000 feet.

The lobby of this alpine inn, called The Ubaye, everything is cozy, overstuffed, and clock-like.

Seated on the sofa, facing the register desk is John Pergolesi, an American-born journalist who was on his way to Hiroshima when he became detoured by the avalanche of tenors. He has been instructed by his Boston/Cambridge family to bring back to the states the body of his aunt.

The table in front of Pergolesi is cluttered with papers, photographs, magazines, and the lenses to John's cameras.

Mrs. Harriet Owings, the 67 year-old proprietress of The Ubaye Inn, enters. She carries a tray with tea and pastries, and places them on the table. She is tall, slender, and has a stubborn beauty to her that has not yet forsaken her. She is dressed quite plainly. At some point we should realize that this part is being played by a man.

MRS. OWINGS: Did you hear the music?

PERGOLESI: Music! ... No, I heard no music.

MRS. OWINGS: Well, there is music in things we do not hear. *(No response.)*

MRS. OWINGS: You do believe that, don't you?

PERGOLESI: Believe in what?

MRS. OWINGS *(Serving the tea)*: There is music in things we do not hear?

PERGOLESI: I am not a poet.

MRS. OWINGS: I would never have guessed.

PERGOLESI: I have just come here to fetch my aunt.

MRS. OWINGS: Well, she's upstairs waiting. Room 24-B.

PERGOLESI: Are there any others?

MRS. OWINGS: Aunts? I'm sure you know more about your own relatives than I do.

PERGOLESI: I mean bodies. Bodies recovered from the rubble.

MRS. OWINGS: A few. But most have been claimed on the other side of the mountain. I only had your aunt brought here because Priscilla was a dear friend of mine. If your family had not made arrangements to have her body shipped home, I would have seen after the funeral arrangements myself.

PERGOLESI: Which would have been very kind of you.

MRS. OWINGS: Yes, I suppose it would have been.

Or you might begin with conflict or strong action that immediately draws in the audience, such as this opening of the play *Marching in Time* by Zachary Thomas:

> *(The curtain opens on a dark stage to the slow beating of a drum that continues under the following dialog. Slowly, the lights come up to reveal a strangely alien landscape, an exterior devoid of any but the most twisted vegetation. Off in the distance an orange sun casts its dying glow. The following is broadcast through loudspeakers throughout the theatre.)*

VOICE ONE: Once upon a *(echo chamber)* time, time, time, time, time, time, time —

VOICE TWO: Ten, nine, eight, seven, six, five, four, three, two, one — *(A clock beats faster and faster and — BOOM, an explosion!)*

VOICE THREE: So students, Einstein stated that space and time are relative. The faster one travels in space, *(Begins to speak very slowly, like a wind-up record player running out of time.)* the more slowly time passes —

VOICE ONE: *(brightly)* What is *Time*? *Time* is a magazine? If you have time, walk to the corner newsstand ...

VOICE TWO: Hup, two, three, four; hup, two, three, four; hup, two, three ...

(A nondescript MAN of an indeterminate age, wearing a pair of rumpled brown coveralls enters Left and strides toward Center. A WOMAN in silver shoes, with silver hair, wearing a silver dress with a silver boa that trails after her, enters Right and strides toward Center. Intent upon continuing on, paying little attention to their surroundings, the MAN and WOMAN nearly collide. They stop and regard each other silently until the MAN finally speaks.)

MAN: I'm afraid I haven't arrived in time —

WOMAN: Of course, you're in time. Everyone —

MAN: I don't understand.

WOMAN: You're afraid the king is dead. You're afraid —

(A Dusenberg convertible with an oogle horn oogling pulls onto the stage. The DRIVER wears a car coat, cap and goggles. He drives erratically, screeching to a halt a foot or two Upstage of the MAN and WOMAN. He disembarks, slamming the door.)

DRIVER: *(Glancing from the MAN to the WOMAN and back again)* The time has come! The instant, the nano-second in the bursting fabric of the universe —

(A dozen soldiers, bayonets drawn, converge from a dozen directions Upstage, Right, Left. They are dressed in camouflage, dead leaves stuck to their helmets, their faces painted brown and green. The SERGEANT wears over his heart a large silver badge that reads SERGEANT. He advances, circles the DRIVER, the MAN and the WOMAN — one time, two times, three times.)

SERGEANT: *(Stopping dead in his tracks)* Time is of the essence, this time. There will be no escape. *(Motioning to his men)* Escort them to the stockade.

ACTIVITIES

1. Come up with two opposing characters and an idea for a play, or continue to work with those you already have decided upon. Write monologs in which each character explains why it is important and logical to reach his or her goal, keeping in mind that the protagonist and the antagonist have goals that directly oppose each other.

2. Now take these two characters, and on the basis of the monologs and anything else you know about them, write a scene in which they are in direct opposition or in conflict.

3. You've decided on your protagonist and his or her goal. Keeping in mind that a play should have meaning for the audience, write a paragraph or two explaining how your character's needs are universal or at least symbolize universality.

4. Keeping your protagonist's goal in mind, write out in paragraph form three or four logical obstacles to that goal, obstacles that the protagonist could or will encounter in the course of your play.

5. Your character's reaching the goal or not depends on the type of person he or she is. As you can see from the character of Regina in *The Little Foxes*, sometimes a protagonist's actions are not admirable; sometimes a person goes too far in trying to squelch others simply for profit. Or sometimes the goal is wrong or illogical, such as Willy's defining success in financial terms and deciding the only way to achieve financial security for his family is to kill himself.

Write out a paragraph explaining whether or not your protagonist is an admirable or "right-thinking" person and why the chosen goal should be pursued. What about your protagonist makes the person likeable and admirable (as is the case with most protagonists) or else hateful or despicable?

6. Take a look at the scene or scenes you've written so far, keeping in mind the idea that in real life and in plays, people rarely are blatant in stating explicitly what they want. Is your character subtle enough? Too subtle? What makes you think so?

7. Write a beginning scene for your play, a scene in which you try your best to hook an audience. Why do you think this is a good hook?

75

CHAPTER 5

Some Basics

To write plays, you need to be acquainted with theatre; the more you know, at least about the practical aspects, the better.

WHAT IS THEATRE?

For purposes of playwriting, you might simply think of theatre as the presentation of a play before a live audience. Yet you can do this in the living room of your house or in an auditorium that seats 1500 or 2000 people.

Perhaps the oldest of the arts, because it involves imitation, theatre more closely approximates life than does anything else, except life itself; the characters "act" the way people do in life. They portray emotions each of us experiences, and they react to life just like we do. Even the setting for a play can look a lot like real life.

As in real life (and any of the other arts, for that matter), theatre's purpose is to communicate. Whether this involves a single actor performing before passersby in the park or an elaborate staged musical, the same basics are present.

Theatre is more specific in its communication than many other arts. It also is more encompassing than a novel, a poem, or a painting because it combines so many elements (architecture and color in setting, lights, costumes, and so on), and is nearly limitless in what it can convey. Because of this, it has greater potential to involve us more personally than some of the other art forms.

A number of characteristics combine to make theatre unique. First, unlike a book or a painting, it is temporal. Each production of a play exists only for a period of time and can never again be witnessed in exactly the same way. Fine arts and novels or poetry, on the other hand, can be enjoyed again and again in exactly the same state.

The same script can be performed time and again, but each performance differs from any other. The director, the designers, and the actors of one production interpret the play differently than do any others. One actor's appearance, movement, and voice differ from those of any other actor who takes the same role. Stages differ in size. Properties and costumes differ from production to production. Each night of a production's run will differ from all the others. The actors continue to grow and change in their roles. Their personal lives or moods may influence one performance more strongly than another.

The vision you have as a playwright will differ from what is produced on the stage. This is because once you finish the script, it is no longer completely yours. You are only one collaborator among many.

PLAYWRIGHT: Hey, you call this collaboration. Well, I don't think so, you know. I mean this isn't how I saw things at all. This isn't what I wanted.

DIRECTOR: What you wanted! What's that got to do with anything? It's my baby now, and what I say goes.

SET DESIGNER: You want what!

DIRECTOR: I told you that the damn platform is too low. We're supposed to be looking up at this guy, baby. How can you look up to someone two inches above the stage floor?

SET DESIGNER: I suppose you spent years studying design, right? So you know what works best. Well, let me tell you —

DIRECTOR: I am the director, and what I say goes.

LIGHTING DESIGNER: How do you expect me to light this set? My God, all these false ceilings and overhangs and —

COSTUMER: Well, damn it, the central character is ethereal, at least that's the way I see it.

PLAYWRIGHT: Ethereal, you're outta your gourd!

COSTUME DESIGNER: Well, I never —

SET DESIGNER: For once the twerp's right.

PLAYWRIGHT: Twerp? Who are you calling a twerp?

SET DESIGNER: *(Ignoring him)* It takes place in a mountain cabin, right? Everything is roughhewn.

DIRECTOR: Then get rid of that damned marble fireplace.

SET DESIGNER: The fireplace! That's the key to the second act —

PLAYWRIGHT: Second act! There's no damned fireplace; I never mentioned a damned fireplace.

DIRECTOR: Well, you know what Guthrie said.

78

SET DESIGNER: Arlo? What's he got to —

DIRECTOR: Not Arlo, you twit. Tyrone, the great English director. Well, he said that the playwright is the least capable of all of judging what he's written. He's the ... channel, whatever. It's up —

PLAYWRIGHT: Channel? Channel! Now let me tell you. *(A LOUD VOICE booms throughout the theatre.)*

LOUD VOICE: I am your producer; you will do as I say. And I say you will stop all this foolish bickering, or I'm going to fire the lot of you. Understood?

LIGHTING DESIGNER: Bickering? We weren't bickering. *(To DIRECTOR)* Were we bickering?

DIRECTOR: We wouldn't do anything like that. Sorry, sir, if it appeared to you that we were bickering. What do the rest of you say? Does it appear to you we were bickering?

ALL: We weren't bickering; we collaborate; that's our job. We get along.

LOUD VOICE: Perhaps I was mistaken. Forgive my intrusion. I only want what's best for the production. I want to make money! But since you weren't bickering — and you say you weren't and I believe you — I probably don't need to say this, but I will. Look, kiddies, any more of this ... this non-bickering, and you're history, got it?

THEATRE IMITATES

Theatre directly imitates human experiences by allowing the spectators to identify with characters who are represented as real, to put themselves in the characters' places and feel as the characters do.

The imitation comes about through the efforts of many people. The playwright, the actors, the director, and the designers all add their own backgrounds and experiences to a production. All these people with diverse backgrounds judge; they overlook; they point out specific emotions and traits to the exclusion of others. They select color and style and shape. Through these choices, they add their own personalities and perceptions of the world. They interpret events and actions in the play from differing viewpoints. All art is subjective, but in theatre a number of viewpoints combine to make the form totally distinctive. Each of the individuals involved contributes something personal to the total production, which then presents life in a many-faceted manner.

In addition to combining viewpoints, theatre encompasses many forms of art. It includes architecture in the setting, sculpture in three-dimensional forms and the use of lights and shadow, dance in the planned movement (blocking), painting in the setting and makeup, literature in the words, and music in songs and the flow of the language. Artists with a variety of backgrounds and training work together to bring about a unified production.

THEATRE AS IMITATION AND RITUAL

How did such a complex form ever begin? Well, most theatre historians think it stemmed from two basic human traits: the *mimetic instinct* and the need for *ritual*.

> **AT RISE:** It is after a great hunt; the mighty HUNTERS have returned to the area of the caves.

IGGY: *(Pointing off into the distance)* **Oh, ding ding ding go es th tro lle y.**

TRANSLATOR: *(Facing the vast audience)* **Me look. Me see big wooly. Big wooly long tooth.**

AGGY: *(Jumping up and down)* **Chi-cha, cha cha, char les-ton, ji tter bu ggg tw is ttt, co ol ma nnn.**

TRANSLATOR: **Him see. Me see. Us see. Big, big, big elephant, hairy toes.**

UGGY: *(Looking at others, grabs up an imaginary rock.)* **Oncea po na ti mein a fa roff kin gdo mmm. Li ve da bee uti fu lpr in cess.**

TRANSLATOR: **Big rock. Hit. Stop big wooly thing. Us now food. Winter long food. It spoil, so what? We still eat.** *(All the HUNTERS grab imaginary rocks and begin to stalk the thing with the big wooly toes. The AUDIENCE sits in rapt attention.)*

Just as primitive people portrayed what was important in their lives, contemporary dramatists, designers and directors usually begin by communicating what they have learned from the world around them. That is, they imitate. Usually the imitation is only a starting point, and the playwright, actors, and designers allow their imaginations free rein.

Psychologists state that each of our new experiences is built upon something we already know. We relate a new situation to our past awareness and thus build our memories and experi- ences. We have certain expectations, which are only slightly altered by new surroundings or new people. Occasionally, we encounter something outside our realm of experience or meet a person to whom we cannot relate, but we use our past as a point of departure in learning or in creativity.

Of course this is what theatre artists do. They explore and, through the art of theatre, present a whole range of thoughts and feelings. So theatre is a way of learning for both artist and audience. It can broaden our cultural and humanistic horizons. It can give us confidence by showing us we are like others, and it can help us explore our individual selves.

WHAT IS DRAMA?

Playwriting or drama probably isn't quite as easy to define as is theatre. But since we defined theatre in part by saying that it's a presentation which is pre-planned, we might consider that the beginning of this pre-planning is the play, which can be a detailed script or, as in the case of improvisation, a bare outline.

STUDENT: *(Obviously a snob)* **Well, it occurs to me then that — ahem — drama is action and dialog, portraying conflict in the form of a story and presented by actors on a stage for the entertainment and/or enlightenment of an audi- ence. In my estimation then, the foregoing certainly should give one —** *(Glancing around the class disdainfully)* **a clearer idea of what drama is.**
PROFESSOR: **What you're saying then is that a guy writes a script, okay?**
STUDENT: *(Nose cocked in the air)* **Precisely.**
PROFESSOR: **And that in this script there is conflict, a plot, so to speak.**
STUDENT: **My point exactly.**
PROFESSOR: **And a bunch of people get together and act out this script and hope the audience enjoys itself and learns something to boot.**

STUDENT: *(Looking from face to face and smiling broadly)* I'm happy, madam, that we agree.

PROFESSOR: Oh, sure, we agree. Except — As everyone reading this book already knows, you're talking about only one kind of play.

STUDENT: *(Puzzled, frowning)* One sort of —? Why, er, uh, I — *(The OTHER STUDENTS snicker.)*

PROFESSOR: You said yourself it tells a story, isn't that right?

STUDENT: *(Confused)* I did ... I mean, didn't I? I mean, isn't that just what I ... I did say it, yes. *(The OTHER STUDENTS guffaw.)*

PROFESSOR: Oh, you aren't wrong ... exactly. You're just talking about one type, the kind that has a plot.

STUDENT: *(Becoming faint)* One type, but I thought ... I mean I stayed up all night reading books, trying to impress you with — I mean ...

PROFESSOR: Oh, don't take it so hard. The one you describe is the most common, the one that's endured throughout history.

STUDENT: May I be excused? Please. I want to read, I want to study, I need books, books. Oh, God, I need to look at some books. *(Trembling violently, s/he rushes from the room.)*

Perhaps we shouldn't be too hard on the student because, as the prof says and you already know, this is the most common type of play (Stay tuned to learn more about it in Chapters 6 and 7). For now, let's just talk more about the fact that the most important consideration of the story play is the idea of conflict and opposition, two forces struggling against each other.

According to Aristotle, author of *The Poetics*, the first important treatise on drama, a play should have a beginning, a middle and an end.

NOT-SO-BRIGHT STUDENT: Well, obviously man, everything that begins has to end. The world has to end, right? Even this damn class has to — Oops. *(Highly embarrassed, he abruptly sits down.)*

PROFESSOR: It's okay. Nobody has to like the class. I mean just because you don't like it, I'm not going to give you an "F," am I? ... *(Muttering to himself)* Oh, yeah, a "D" minus but not an "F." *(Resuming his professorial tones)*

What Aristotle meant was that a play should be complete in itself. Unlike old movie serials or soap operas, it should contain everything necessary for the audience to understand it in its entirety. *(Looking at NOT-SO-BRIGHT-STUDENT)* **It should be "all there," in other words, unlike certain students who ...**

Aristotle also meant that a play should have a cause-to-effect relationship, with the dramatic question (or problem) introduced early on and then resolved before the ending. He stated that the play should be an "imitation of an *action*." The central character meets an obstacle and tries to overcome it. The action continues until the tragic hero is defeated or the problem resolved.

An audience at a play has to have a sense of ending, a feeling of completion. Even if a play has no plot the spectators have to feel either a sense of satisfaction or a sense of emotional release at the last-act curtain.

Audiences also want a play to mean something, so it has to be selective, free of unimportant details of action and speech. Characters cannot be fully explored (in any art form really), and time is compressed. A playwright selects the high points or the moments of direct conflict and omits extraneous material.

Often directors or actors will say in reference to a script: "It plays better than it reads." They mean that an audience cannot receive the full impact of a play by reading it silently. They need the atmosphere of a theatre and the technical aspects of the stage performance. Some scripts even seem drab or uninteresting when read silently. Yet when the set designer adds a visual interpretation, the actors analyze and impersonate the characters, and the director integrates the total production, the script only then fully communicates the playwright's intention. In this way theatre or any other "temporal" art form like opera or dance, is different from forms that continue to exist in an unchanged state, even vastly different from those that use characters and words and conflict.

The major difference between theatre and other forms of storytelling is that theatre "shows," while short stories, novels and oral storytelling often rely on narration.

A novel is much longer than a play, relies on long passages of description to fill in the exposition or background material, whereas a play is brief and relies on what the audience sees and hears.

Fiction has the usual convention of being written in the "past," which the reader, of course, accepts as the present. (Of course, some novels and short stories do occur in the present, which, incidentally, many readers find disturbing because it breaks the usual rules). Theatre operates in a continuous "present."

A novel often deals with a character's whole life, while a play rarely does. This is because novels can take much longer — many hours to read, for instance — while the usual play (*Mourning Becomes Electra* or *Nicholas Nickleby* notwithstanding) takes no more than a couple of hours onstage.

THEATRE CONVENTIONS

STUDENT: You mean if I major in theatre, I'll get to go to conventions and meetings in all those great places like Vegas and Orlando and New York City and — Wow, I'm so excited! I always wanted —

PROFESSOR: *(Laughing professorially)* Ho, ho, ho. Of course, you may get to do that. There are theatre organizations and such that hold this sort of meeting. But that isn't exactly what Cassady means by the heading — at least I don't think that's what he means. *(Aside)* You don't, do you?

A theatre piece relies on particular devices (conventions) that the actors, the playwright, the designers, or the director use to expedite the production. An audience willingly accepts and expects such devices as a type of shorthand.

According to Samuel Taylor Coleridge, a nineteenth-century poet and critic, theatre involves "the willing suspension of disbelief." Those working on the production of a play attempt to create an illusion of reality, which the audience is willing to accept as real.

Most theatrical conventions involve selectivity. Often they imply rather than show or state something. In old-fashioned "meller"dramas, for instance, we know immediately who the villain is because he dresses in black and constantly twists the ends of his moustache.

An audience at a play accepts such conventions as actors projecting their voices to be heard throughout the auditorium or rarely turning their backs on the spectators (at least in a proscenium theatre), or using broader gestures in a large theatre than they normally would in everyday life.

The spectator isn't bothered that the living room on stage is really made up of a series of flats, that furniture is arranged differently in a real living room, or that the living room on stage is much larger than the one in most homes.

Audiences know that what appears to be real is not. A diamond ring may be a piece of costume jewelry. A letter is only a piece of blank paper. A pistol fires blanks. Lighting is artificial sunlight or moonlight, and there are more shadows in real life than on stage. The lights on stage are brighter than those we use at home, and they illuminate a larger area. The audience knows, too, that an actor usually wears more makeup than does the person on the sidewalk.

As a playwright, you have to be aware of various conventions you can and should use. Most are concerned with heightening and condensing, with choosing high points.

Some playwriting conventions are the monolog, the soliloquy and the flashback. All are ways of presenting exposition or background information (a convention in itself) and feelings. A soliloquy shows a character thinking aloud, in much the same way we may talk to ourselves when we are alone. It succinctly reveals a character's inner feelings. Without the use of such conventions, we would have to include many more scenes in a play.

Similar is the sort of monolog in which a character speaks directly to the audience, as does the Stage Manager in *Our Town*, when he describes Grover's Corners, New Hampshire. Or when one character speaks to others, mostly to reveal feelings and thoughts.

Flashbacks are similar to soliloquies or monologs in that they can provide exposition necessary to the audience's understanding of events, conditions or characters. A flashback is a "scene" that occurred before the play's action begins. Most often the audience members are asked to imagine that they can "see" what a character is thinking as the remembered scene appears on stage. Arthur Miller's *Death of a Salesman* contains a number of flashbacks, including the times when Willie imagines Biff and Happy are young again.

Events progress faster on the stage that they do in real life. Characters express their thoughts more explicitly and concisely than do people in everyday life. They leave out unnecessary and distracting details, which ordinarily intrude on conversations.

Action is condensed. In Sophocles' *Oedipus Rex*, for example, we learn all the events that preceded the action of the play from Oedipus' infancy to marrying his mother; yet the play takes place in less than a day's time.

As a playwright, you should know that an audience will accept almost any character or event if it is in the proper framework. For instance, Shakespeare introduces ghosts and witches into his plays. Karel Čapek used robots in *R.U.R.* The audience is willing to accept these devices because a framework has been established in which they can exist. Only when the author deviates from that framework does a play become unbelievable.

LEARNING TO KNOW THEATRE

It is difficult to become a playwright if you know nothing about theatre or haven't worked around it. Throughout the writing and revising of a script, you need to consider whether what you are writing is practical to produce. When there is a scene change, you need to know enough about scenery to make such a change possible without great difficulty.

You should know enough about the styles of production to be able to determine what will work best for the play you are writing. It helps to visualize how a play can be presented, so that you can write something that truly is producible.

If you have not already done so, hang around whatever theatres are available — community, educational, professional. Most theatres are glad to have volunteer help in many areas.

Get on the set construction crew so you will see how platforms and flats and step units are built. See how they are managed and how actors use them.

Learn about how scenery can be shifted and about the

functions and use of lighting. If possible, act in a play, even in a minor role, to get a feel for what it's like.

Learn about the different types of stages, and the stage areas and how to hang lights and run sound. The more familiar you are with theatre, the more you are likely to write a practical and easily executed script.

Most plays are written for a proscenium stage so that you need to know about the areas of the stage to describe them and write directions. This will give you an idea:

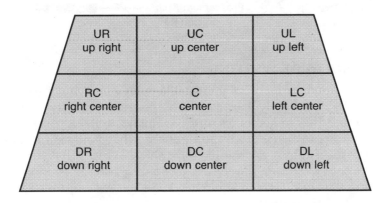

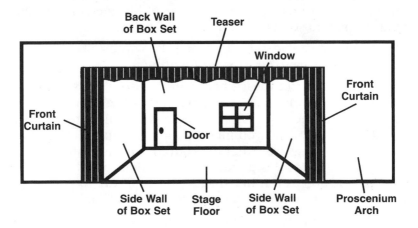

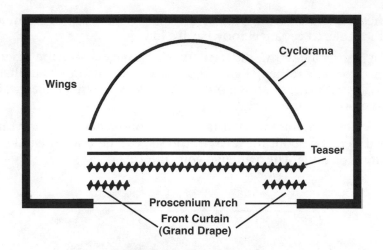

SOME RULES OF WRITING

First, of course, you should like plays and theatre. You should be thoroughly familiar with the genre of playwriting. You should like to see plays and read plays. But more so, you should learn to be discriminating about what you see or read. What sorts of things do you like or dislike? Why? What could a playwright have done differently to make a play more interesting or believable? How could the characters be improved, the basic plot, the conflict?

A few years ago a writer who attended a workshop I conducted started to read scenes from one of his screen plays. One week he had no scene to read. "Why?" I asked.

"Well," he answered, "if anyone else wrote a play like that, I'd never go to see it. So why am I writing it?"

You have to like theatre and drama to write plays. You have to like the particular play you're writing — the characters, the plot, the idea, the style. Oh, I suppose you could write plays if you didn't like to, and you might do a good job. All of us have had to write things we didn't like. But in this case, why bother? So if you decide at this point, you really don't want to write a play, maybe don't even like theatre, rush quickly to your nearest used bookstore with this book; do not pass "go."

To write a play, most of the rules are the same as for any other type of writing. Here are a few. Later chapters will deal more completely with some of these.

1. Don't include characters with similar names like Jerry, Jilly, Jimmy, Johnny. That sort of thing is bad enough when you're reading it in a novel or short story. But at least there you have the advantage of going back and trying to figure out who is who — that is, if by that time, you even care.

2. Remember that all the characters are unique and should speak differently. That is, no character should use the same style, word choice, delivery and so on as any other character. Each style should reflect the character's personality and background. (There will be more on this in Chapter 10, DIALOG.)

3. Unless it is very clear that you are not doing so, you should tell things in sequence, particularly in dialog, or the audience most likely will be confused. For instance, don't say something like:

CHARACTER: I was supposed to go meet Zach downtown. We had talked about it on the phone the previous evening, and he said, "Oh, you know how I like the Taco Store." So I called a cab, which was about fifteen minutes late. When I got out of bed, I knew it was going to be that kind of day. I couldn't find the dress I wanted. So the taxi was late, and the driver got lost along the way.

4. It's better not to put too much information into one speech. For instance:

FRIEND: Man, what happened? You look like a ghost.
CHARACTER: I was scared, you know. Really damned scared. This man broke into the house. A young guy, ski mask, long blond hair. I mean, I heard some noise. It woke me, I guess. The guy was going to kill us. I'm convinced of it. I keep this gun by my bed. In a little table. I grabbed for it, and it was good I did. He was coming into the bedroom. A butcher knife in his hand. He was going to slit our throats or something, I suppose. Anyhow, he saw the gun and dived for the door. I heard him run outside. Someone was waiting, I guess. I heard a car take off. By the time I got to the window the street

was empty. It was then I looked around and saw everything was gone. He stole everything, and I mean everything. The computer, the television, all the other electronic stuff, silverware, jewelry. A ring that belonged to my dad.

This sort of thing ruins the impact of the scene, and it's just plain boring. It's much more suspenseful to stretch it out.

FRIEND: Man, what happened? You look like a ghost.
CHARACTER: I was scared, you know. Really damned scared.
FRIEND: What happened?
CHARACTER: This man broke into the house.
FRIEND: Man? What man?
CHARACTER: A young guy, ski mask, long blond hair.
FRIEND: My God! What did you do?
CHARACTER: It woke me, I guess.
FRIEND: Jeez, Paul. That's awful.
CHARACTER: The guy was going to kill us. I'm convinced of that.
FRIEND: Kill you!

Certainly, there are times when you'll have long speeches, but, as you know, usually their purpose is to explain feelings, not events.

5. Passive voice should be avoided. What I mean is: Don't use passive voice! That isn't an absolute, but it's a good general rule. If you're talking about an auto accident, then use it. For instance, say, "Jack was in an accident; his legs were crushed, his back broken."

Don't say, "Peter Matthews crushed Jack's legs today. He broke his back too." Well, say it if Peter did it deliberately, but then it certainly wouldn't be an accident.

Active voice is more direct, more immediate. It involves the audience. An audience hearing passive voice cannot feel any involvement because the event is over and done with. It isn't an ongoing thing:

Active: Someone smashed all the windows in my car.

Passive: The windows in my car were all broken out.

The former involves us; the latter is like saying, "Last year there were thirty-one days in January." So what?

Incidentally, forget all the rules of this sort if your character is the type who speaks this way. I have a friend who does this, and it drives me nuts!

6. Of course, again, you need to consider your character, but another general rule is: vary sentence types and structure. The following, of course, is exaggerated but shows what I mean.

Don't say: You know I went home last month. Daddy had called and told me Mom was ill. He said her arthritis was terrible. She couldn't get around anymore. I was scared, really scared. She'd always been such a vital person. She'd always been so alive. I was expecting the worst. I drove past the house. She was mowing the lawn by hand. I couldn't believe it."

Do say: When Daddy called and said Mom's arthritis was so bad she couldn't get around, I was scared. Really scared of seeing her like that. She was always such a vital person, so alive. So I drove past the house, expecting the worst. And what do I see? Mom, cutting the grass with an old push mower. Can you believe it?"

7. This also depends to a degree on the character and how he or she would talk, but usually you should avoid "helper" or "to be" verbs in dialog. It's much more powerful to say, "Rain slammed against the house," than to say, "Rain was slamming against the house."

8. When one of your characters is talking, have the person home in on time and place and be specific. It's much more interesting to an audience.

Don't say: My cousin's always late. It drives me nuts. Even when she was a bridesmaid at her sister's wedding, we barely made it. And I got talked into taking her somewhere again. I can't believe I let that happen.

Do say: My cousin's always late. Like the time I was picking her up to go to her sister's wedding. It's 8:30 in the morning. We gotta drive about 200 miles. The wedding's at 2 o'clock. I get to her house and she isn't even up. So I ring the bell and pound on the door for ten minutes. Finally, she sticks her head out the window and says, "Oh, it's you." Like who else was she expecting? And guess what? Now I let myself get talked into taking her to Rachel's birthday party. I must be nuts. We have an hour, you know, like sixty minutes, to get to the other side of the county, and Beth is still in the shower!

9. Cut useless details. Ask yourself if the dialog is necessary to move the story ahead, to set the mood, to reveal character or to provide needed background information. If not, skip it.

10. Show your characters in action; this is much better than having ten scenes where other people talk about the person.

11. Unless your character is a stuffy person or there are other mitigating circumstances, use contractions, such as "don't" for "do not" and "he's" for "he is."

12. Don't keep using direct address. At first it's annoying, and then it becomes silly.

TED: Hi, Katy.
KATY: Hi, Ted.
TED: How are you feeling today, Katy?
KATY: Fine, Ted. How about you?
TED: I'm good. So, Katy, tell me, are you ready for this
    meeting?
KATY: As ready as I'll ever be, Ted. How about you?
TED: Oh, yeah, Katy, I think so.
KATY: That's good, Ted.

13. People usually don't talk in complete sentences, where everything is fully stated and nothing left to implication:

TED: Did it take a lot of hours for you to prepare your report?
KATY: Yes, it took many hours. How long did it take you?
TED: It took me about seven hours. That's all right, however.
    I think it's worth it if we can land the account.
KATY: Oh, yes, I think so too. It will be good for the
    company and good for us personally.
TED: I couldn't have said it better myself.

14. Instead, say something like:

TED: Take long to do the report?
KATY: A while. How about you?
TED: A good seven hours. But that's okay. It's worth it if we
    can land the account.
KATY: Yeah, for the company *and* for us.
TED: Amen!

15. Work background exposition in gradually. Don't pre-

sent a lot of details at once that don't move the story along. Some things are important for the audience to know near the beginning of a play; others can wait till later. Decide which is which and write them accordingly.

16. Be sure the sentences fit the mood. In active moods, such as excitement or anger, people tend to speak in shorter and choppier sentences. In unemotional moments or times of contentment or relaxation, the sentences tend to be longer and more flowing.

17. Be sure to set the proper tone at the beginning of the play. Don't mislead the audience into thinking a serious play is going to be funny or vice versa. This has a lot to do with sentence structure and flow of language.

18. Don't repeat words close together unless you do it for a specific effect.

Don't say: "I went outside today, and saw that the day was dreary. I knew I was going to have a bad day at work."

Do say: "It was a bad day, the worst kind of day I could imagine."

19. Don't include in stage directions what should go in dialog. Don't write: *(ALL say they're sorry.)* Rather write:

JOHN: I'm sorry, man. I wouldn't have had this happen for anything.
RUTH: My sympathies, Matt. It's so unfair.
PETE: A terrible thing, Matt. What can I say?

20. Some plays have narrators, but generally this is not a good thing. If you have to rely on a narrator to provide exposition and bridges between scenes, most often you're in trouble.

21. Plot your play; plan it out! Don't just go from Point A to Point B without building conflict and tension. You need a central problem. Don't just have a series of incidents that don't lead anywhere. There are exceptions, but it's better first to learn the "tried and true."

ACTIVITIES

1. What rituals do we engage in today in our society? How can you apply these to theatre?

93

2.   All art, as you know, has restrictions. What are some of theatre's restrictions, those not mentioned in the chapter?

3.   Can you think of other playwriting or theatre conventions that are not listed in the chapter?

4.   List any other rules of writing that apply to writing in general or to playwriting in particular.

CHAPTER 6

Dramatic Structure

A story play has a plot.

Plot is structure.

Structure is conflict.

Neither plot nor structure is the story.

Q: **Oh, really? Aren't they the same?**
A: **No, they are not. They spring from the same location, just as your thumb comes from your hand, which comes from your arm, which comes from your body.**

The body is the universe; the arm is the world; the hand is the plot; the thumb and fingers are a bunch of digits which interact with each other.

Let's talk about the thumb. It has several sides. One is covered with a "finger" print, and has a few creases, two in particular that are predominant. Curving around from this underside are two relatively smooth sides, which nevertheless differ from each other. One has a wider curve, for instance, from the tip to the first knuckle.

The back of the thumb, the part that is revealed to me the most, has lines that are modified arcs, a cuticle, a thumbnail and so on.

Although this is the side of my own thumb I see most often, sometimes I see the other sides as well, although that's not the ordinary state of affairs. My thumb opposes my fingers — sometimes just one of them, sometimes several at once.

My thumb is my central character, my hero, my protagonist — so far as my hand goes. The fingers, sometimes one at a time, sometimes working in conjunction with each other, are the single or collective antagonist, the force that opposes my thumb.

If I wear a long-sleeved shirt, the fingers and hand are all that appear to exist, i.e., they are the only visible parts.

Sometimes, my sleeve slips up and reveals a part of my arm. At other times, I roll back my shirt sleeves a couple of folds, and *voila*, I see part of the "thing" that supports my plot and my characters.

My hand contains my characters; it has structure. It is plot. My hand could not exist as a moving, working entity if it were separated from my arm. But as part of my arm, it does move.

My arm supports my hand. My arm is the world. Sometimes I have tendinitis, which affects my arm (the world) and my hand (the plot) so that my thumb and fingers (the characters in my play) are harder to move. Maybe it's like there's been a natural disaster that has played havoc with civilization, or maybe it's a terrible illness that may kill the population (my fingers).

The conditions of the world — my tendinitis or a bruise, a strain, a cut — affect my hand.

My world (my arm) is part of my body, which is the universe. This too affects my plot and my characters. And certainly it affects my world (arm).

My body and my arm are the framework that supports my plot, which does most of the work in flexing the wrist and moving the characters.

Without my body (the universe), there would be no world. Without my arm (the world) there would be no plot or movement (my hand), and without movement, my characters (my fingers) are as good as dead.

When things are going smoothly, my fingers and thumb work together to type this page of text. Sometimes one of them rebels and makes a tuping error. "Tuping?" Well, what did I tell you!

But generally in the world of my characters (my fingers and thumb) things run pretty smoothly. Sometimes, though, there is stress; sometimes there is conflict and opposition. In a hand, that's okay, because the opposition supports whatever I pick up. It helps me reach the goal of moving my typed chapter from the printer to the table beside me.

Characters opposing each other are okay too. In fact they are essential to plot and to story. Without them, the plot would never unfold. Oh, sure there could be a story involving my other hand. But that's entirely different. It's sinister; it's alien; it's a parallel world where everything is opposite. It's like entering into a black hole where time runs backwards and everything is made (or not made?) of anti-matter.

The point of all this is that a plot is not an isolated thing. It's a part of much, much more. It encompasses "everything" known and unknown.

FRAME OF REFERENCE

What all the foregoing means is that a play cannot exist as an isolated entity that springs into existence on November 10, 1882, at 1 p.m. and ends November 13, 1882 at 3 a.m.

A story play — sometimes called a well-made play or a cause-to-effect play — doesn't suddenly spring up out of the mists of some unknown somewhere or sometime; when it ends, the characters, the setting — in our imaginations, at least — don't suddenly trail off into mist.

There is a framework, which is all the conditions of the world and universe. Most of these aren't mentioned, of course, because they do not directly affect the action.

If the framework, however, is alien (my left hand), more conditions have to be explained. In this new world, the people breathe mercury instead of oxygen. They use a complicated barter system consisting of "obs," obligations, to see to their needs and pleasures.

They have no wars; instead, when they are eight years old (that's seventeen years old, our time), they face each other across a complicated game board.

The winner dies, but he brings honor to his family. The loser, after a year of dressing in fine robes and anthracite jewelry and holding his head high in terrible shame, goes back to dressing in the usual plant forms that everyone else wears...

The more vastly different from our own world and time the universe you create for your play, the more explaining you need to do. Otherwise, the audience will be totally confused. (With such a scenario as the one above, maybe they're confused anyhow!)

CHILD: Tell me a story, Dad. You promised.
DAD: All right, but then you have to go to sleep, okay?

CHILD: Okay.

DAD: Once upon a time in a far off kingdom lived a handsome prince who decided to seek a bride. In order to find the fairest young woman in the land, he decided to hold ...

Kids love stories; they have no trouble accepting a time and place where a handsome prince decides to invite all the young women of the kingdom to his palace. They do as Coleridge suggested and willingly suspend their disbelief.

However, once the disbelief is suspended, the created universe and world and plot that results cannot change.

DAD: ... to find the fairest young woman in the land, he decided to hold a big party at this disco in downtown Philadelphia!

CHILD: No, Daddy! No, that's not the way the story goes. He decided to hold a ball. Don't you know what a ball is?

DAD: Sure, something you shoot baskets with.

CHILD: Daddyyyyy! I want to hear the story about how the prince invited everyone to the ball and how poor Cinderella was treated so mean by her stepsisters and —

Once a framework is established — no matter how fanciful or magical — you cannot change it and keep your audience.

Is Karel Čapek's *R.U.R.* really believable? Will robots take over the earth someday? Are there really ghosts and witches such as appear in Shakespeare's *Hamlet* and *Macbeth*?

The playwrights have set forth a certain frame of reference in each. They have created a world in which these elements can exist. Yet Arthur Miller in writing *Death of a Salesman* probably never considered having a robot bail Willy out of his financial troubles. A certain framework was established, and an audience would be unwilling to suspend its disbelief beyond that framework. Miller built a framework that was close to the everyday situation many Americans might encounter. Yet he did present expository material through the technique of flashbacks which the audience was willing to accept even though they had to imagine they were privileged to witness the workings of Willy Loman's mind. Čapek depicted a society in which robots did

98

exist. The two playwrights presented frameworks that were believable. Once they were established, the audience was willing to suspend its disbelief so that the inclusion of unusual or bizarre events didn't shock them. It's only when a particular framework exists and then the author deviates from it that the play becomes unbelievable.

The framework is the setup, and once it's established it's absolute. From then on, a play sticks to:

   a. a specific action or actions

   b. a specific time or times

   c. a specific place or places

all within this absolute framework. The questions are:

   a. *What* is happening?

   b. *When* is it happening?

   c. *Where* is it happening?

Everyone likes stories. We find them in magazines, books, tapes, film, television, theatre, at oral storytelling events, performance pieces. Basically, the stories are the same kinds of things in all these media. They deal with people, events, times, problems, feelings, themes. Yet, they most often hold our attention because of their plot and characters.

A story play, a conventional piece of fiction, the usual movie or dramatic/comic television series or special involves a clash of forces or wills.

Somebody has to win. Which will it be, the "good guy," who is called the protagonist, or the "bad guy," called the antagonist?

Except that the good guy isn't always good, but merely the central character.

The bad guy isn't always bad, but merely has differing views, for instance, in alphabetical order:

Democrat versus Republican

(or) Republican versus Democrat

The plot shows the struggle between the protagonist and the antagonist until one of them wins, and the other is defeated.

George Bush versus Bill Clinton

Did the good guy win, or did the bad guy win?

What if they're all bad guys, like Regina and her greedy brothers in *The Little Foxes*. Well, usually it's the protagonist or central character that we want to win. Most of the time we identify with this person; we empathize and sympathize. But we don't have to.

Sometimes, we want the protagonist to lose, but that is unusual.

Remember the thumb and the hand and the arm? Sometimes the thumb and the index finger are opposed, sometimes it's the thumb and another finger or fingers.

The same is true in a story play. The protagonist most often is an individual, though in rare cases it is a group of people:

Mob of Rabbits Attacks Farmer McGregor

GARDEN PATCH (USA). In late breaking news, county extension agent and part-time reporter Timothy Hayseed tells us that a mob of fluffy cottontails, acting as a single entity with no perceptible leader, early this morning attacked Farmer McGregor as he left his barn carrying a pail of milk.

The bunnies, carrying rotten colored eggs, pelted McGregor till he was smelly, sulphurous mass of dripping, yellow slime. Please watch later editions for updates.

Probably the most familiar case of a group protagonist is the Weavers in Gerald Hauptmann's play *The Weavers*.

Although the protagonist almost always is an individual, the antagonist can be another person, a group of people or a non-individualized force.

TYPES OF OPPOSITION

There are five general types of opposition, the protagonist against:

(1) *another person*

(2) *self*

(3) *society*

(4) *the forces of nature*

(5) *fate*

An example of the first is Anthony Shaffer's *Sleuth*, a two-character melodrama in which the two men constantly try to outwit each other and gain the upper hand.

Sometimes a play pitting one person against another has a simple plot and doesn't go deeply into character, but that is not always the case. Shaffer's play relies a great deal on deception and one-upmanship.

Here are a couple of examples of *a person against self*:

In *Death of a Salesman*, Willy Loman tries to live up to his own definition of success.

In *Oedipus Rex*, Oedipus struggles against his own sense of pride to prove he is not the killer of his father, though it becomes clearer and clearer throughout the play that he is.

A *person against society* or a particular segment of society is one of the most common types of opposition. Ibsen, for instance, often used this sort of situation:

In *Ghosts* Mrs. Alving had been forced to stay with a totally dissolute husband. After his death, she has built an orphanage to honor him and so hide his true character. All her efforts to escape what Alving was fail because her son Oswald has inherited a venereal disease from his father.

Stockman in *An Enemy of the People* battles an entire town when he wants to close the polluted baths, which, however, are the villagers main source of income.

Many plays deal with a person's having to overcome early circumstances and rise above them.

The following, though not a play, is an excellent example

of a *person against nature.*

In Jack London's short story, *To Build a Fire*, a man is trapped in freezing temperatures and tries to light a fire so he won't freeze to death. This story is realistic and filled with drama.

The problem is that often this type of plot comes across as overly melodramatic. No matter how many times poor Job in the Bible tries to rise above his circumstances, he's beaten down again and again, through no fault of his own. In other words, he has no control over what happens. This is often the case in plays about a person versus nature (or the gods).

Many times, however, the conflict only superficially is between the protagonist and the force. Often it's the character against self in the reaction to the flood or drought, so that the person's mettle is tested, and he or she learns a great deal about self.

Or in battling nature, the protagonist may simply be coming up against another obstacle in a different sort of struggle. An example is Eliza's attempting to get across the ice in George Aikin's dramatization of Harriet Beecher Stowe's *Uncle Tom's Cabin*. At the moment of her flight, the ice is a hindrance, yet it is people or conditions that brought about the institution of slavery that she is trying to escape.

A *person versus fate* is equally difficult to make convincing in that it often seems that the protagonist is being controlled without any sense of freedom. Superficially, Brian Clark's *Who's Life Is this Anyway?*, which deals with the right-to-die issue, is based on a protagonist versus fate in that the leading character is dying. But it's really a struggle against society, or accepted standards. Although it was fate that left Helen Keller deaf and blind, it is her struggle against her own stubbornness and self-centeredness that forms the basis of the conflict in *The Miracle Worker*. Of course, Helen often strikes out at Annie Sullivan, but it is really herself she is battling.

PLOT

Background (or framework) plus plot equals story play. But what is plot? It is composed of *inciting incident, rising action* (which includes a series of *minor crises*), a *changing or turning point* and a *climax*, all of which add up to "plot."

ELEMENTS OF PLOT

In everyone's life, if it's running smoothly (the ideal), there is a balance:

Of course, one of the two kids on the seesaw is going to shove off the ground or bounce up and down, and the balance is upset. First one side goes up and down and then the other.

Something happens to disturb the peace or evenness of life for the protagonist, something initiated by the antagonist. This is the *inciting incident*.

Someone knocks us down (the inciting incident). We try to get up, and the other person shoves us down once more. This time we leap to our feet and chase him around the corner of a tall building. He sneaks up behind us and knocks us down again. All this is the *rising action*.

The rising action is where the intensity continues to build till it can go no further without the protagonist or antagonist winning. In a comedy the protagonist wins; in a tragedy the antagonist wins.

If an antagonist suddenly appeared and pushed us down, and then we jumped up and knocked him out, this wouldn't be much of a play or a story. It would end too quickly. It would be too easy for the protagonist.

So there are all these other things happening, the six Cs. They are:

Contact (inciting incident): The antagonist knocks us down.

Conflict: We fight back.

Complication (almost invariably more than one): We jump up and chase the antagonist.

A minor *crisis* follows where the antagonist runs around the building, and we're pretty sure we've frightened him away (which results in a minor climax). But he comes up behind us and at least for the time being again gains the upper hand.

Changing (or turning) point: We corner the antagonist, and both of us know it is only a matter of time until he is defeated. The turning point then is where the action can go no further without something irrevocable happening.

Climax: We defeat the antagonist.

All that's left is the *falling action* or *denouement* which draws the play to its conclusion; it shows how things have changed as a result of the climax.

In simplest terms, this is the formula:

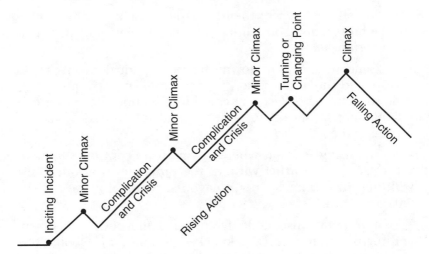

An example of a simple plot occurs in *The Fantasticks*, off-Broadway's longest running musical ever. Matt and Luisa fall in love and are prepared to live happily ever after. But there is a complication. The second act opens with each of them being dissatisfied and feeling a need to experience life before settling down.

Sleuth has many more complications (each resulting in a minor climax where one side appears to be winning), perhaps comparable to a fencing match where first one person attacks and drives back the other; then the second attacks and drives back the first, over and over again until one is declared the victor.

So actually, a plot looks more like this.

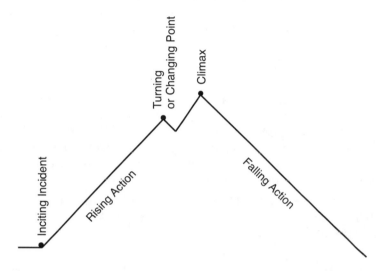

Sometimes the changing point and the climax are the same; at other times they are separated. In Joan Schankar's *The Universal Wolf*, for instance, Grandmother decides to kill Little Red Riding Hood because she can no longer stand her whiny voice. If she had done it immediately after making the decision, the changing point and the climax would have occurred at the same time. Instead, Grandmother sings Little Red Riding Hood to sleep with a lullaby before stabbing her repeatedly with knitting needles.

A play's climax begins to show the answer to the question asked when the problem was introduced; the falling action completes the answer, often explaining more fully how and why a thing happened, or showing the effects of the resolution on the characters. It ties up all the loose ends. In a comedy, the audience wants to enjoy the protagonist's triumph with him or her.

If the protagonist is defeated, the audience wants to feel the emotions felt by the other characters as a result. In *Death of a Salesman*, the requiem scene shows how Willy's suicide affects the others.

Or suppose a man becomes separated from his family dur-

105

ing wartime. As soon as possible, he begins searching for them. The audience experiences his fears, apprehensions and despair and the fruitless bursts of hope. He discovers a promising clue and follows it through, finding where his family lives. He rushes there and flings open the door. The problem has been resolved and the action completed. But the audience has suffered with the man; now they want to witness the reunion, to rejoice with him and feel his happiness.

In most contemporary plays, the inciting incident occurs either at the beginning of the play or even before it has started. It raises a question that needs to be answered before the play can end. During the *rising action* the protagonist's problem is intensified through a series of complications. The suspense increases. Will the protagonist triumph or be defeated?

In Hellman's *The Little Foxes*, Regina comes up against one obstacle after another in her desire to make a lot of money quickly and easily.

Along with her brothers, she wants to raise funds to establish a cotton mill in their small town. She writes her husband Horace, in a Baltimore hospital with a heart ailment, to send the necessary money. He refuses, which is the first complication and crisis. Next she sends their daughter Alexandra to bring him home. He still refuses her money, which encompasses the second climax and crisis. In the meantime the brothers steal securities belonging to Horace in order to cut Regina out of the scheme. Horace knows about this but refuses to confront them.

However, when he discovers how vindictive and unscrupulous his wife is, he has a heart attack, and Regina refuses to give him his medication. He dies, which ends another complication and crisis. Then she blackmails her brothers into promising her seventy-five percent of the profits.

Sometimes a play contains scenes where there appears to be no direct conflict between the protagonist and antagonist. Yet if the play is well-written, the conflict is inherent; it relates to what already has been shown. For example, one character may be talking to another and describing his or her problem. In so doing, the character may begin to see a solution more clearly or even to clarify his or her own thoughts about the situation.

106

Suppose a journalist is having trouble at the newspaper where he works. A co-worker has accused him of plagiarism in a series of award-winning features he has written. The co-worker even states that he has proof of what the protagonist has done.

The protagonist, Mike Samuels, suspects that one of his ex-girlfriends has agreed to testify against him, to say that the notes for the original articles were stolen from her.

Mike is afraid of losing his job. Maybe in discussing the situation with his wife, he figures out a way of exposing the co-worker once and for all. The audience knows the conflict is present, that it's inherent in the action, yet it comes across indirectly.

This sort of scene may show a part of the character's personality not apparent in scenes with co-workers. It may reveal the way the protagonist's mind works or show what he is planning to do. Thus it builds suspense and anticipation.

Every scene in a story play should relate to the dramatic problem or conflict, the protagonist's attempt to reach the goal. Hamlet's "To be or not to be" soliloquy shows no direct action but only what the character is thinking. Yet it bears directly on what he decides and also reveals character.

DRAMATIC ACTION

Everything that occurs in a play has to be relevant to the advancement of the plot.

Most of what is relevant is made up of dramatic action. Dramatic action exists for three reasons.

1. Most important, it relates to the struggle between the protagonist and antagonist and often results in a direct clash between the two.

Dramatic action is not the same as physical movement. In fact, it can occur with no physical movement whatsoever. There is another soliloquy in which Hamlet decides to kill his uncle. He contemplates killing Claudius at prayer, but decides that then he would go to heaven. Instead, Hamlet will kill him "when he is drunk asleep, or in his rage" or at a similar time so "that his soul may be as damn'd and black as hell."

2. It can help individualize a character, revealing traits that may be important to the later action. For instance, a char-

107

acter who is irritable in little ways may later direct a burst of temper at someone else.

This is called *foreshadowing* and lays the groundwork for what comes later, making it believable and logical. To paraphrase playwright Anton Chekhov:

> If you introduce a gun into the early part of a play, you had better use it before the end of the play.

Don't have characters do something that has no bearing on the play's outcome.

Dramatic action must relate in some way to the protagonist, even if he or she isn't present.

Protagonists initiate an action which in turn affects them. They must be answerable for what they do. They must be affected by their behavior.

Dramatic action involves a clash of forces and is reciprocal, like everyday communication.

YOU: Hi, John, how you doin'?
FRIEND: Can't complain.

You speak to friends, they usually answer. But if you argue...

YOU: You sure as hell can complain if you want to, man.
FRIEND: Wow, you know, I can't believe this. All I did was answer your stupid question.

...you can expect an argument back.

If you are talking to a group in a formal situation, they usually don't answer directly. But if they clear their throats a lot, you know you're in trouble.

And if they scowl and cross their arms over their chests, like Farmer McGregor, you'd better watch out for rotten eggs.

3. Dramatic action also helps create atmosphere.

GROUCH: It was a dark and stormy night.
POLLYANNA: Yes, but now in the glorious light of early morning, I see a wondrous haze of gold all across the meadow.
FARMER: And the corn. Well, it's jest about as high as the

shoulder of yonder giraffe. And if it keeps on agrowin', you know, I think it's going to reach clean up there to the heavens.

GROUCH: Yeah, Pol, baby, there's a golden haze all right. Leftover smoke from those danged fire-breathing dragons.

POLLYANNA: But we have to look on the bright side. Now we have all those roasting ears, all roasted and nice.

FARMER: Well, like I was saying, that corn is mighty, mighty high. But we'd be fools to go out there among all the griffins and werewolves and zombies and climb the cornstalks —

POLLYANNA: But don't you see, Mr. Farmer, they got a right to live, just like you and I do. Just like Grouch does too.

GROUCH: Well, listen up and listen up good. We all made a mistake in coming here. This place is nothin' but brimstone and evil and things that go bump in the —

POLLYANNA: OOOh, do you hear it? Suddenly, there comes a rapping, as of someone gently tapping.

FARMER: My God, it's Lenore. Gone all these many months. Lenore, Lenore!

GROUCH: No, no, for God's sake, man, don't open the door!

POLLYANNA: It's a poor little birdie, all confused and flying into the glass. I'm going to rescue the poor little birdie.

GROUCH: Nooooo! *(POLLYANNA flings open the window.)*

ALL: *(in unison)* Aaaaaaarghhh! Gasp. Gasp. Ugh. *(An ominous silence descends.)*

The short scene provides a lot of information through the reference to specific players. Of course the description of the stage at the beginning would help more in establishing the time and place, but we don't really need it to begin to appreciate the situation.

In the next chapter we'll continue the discussion of plot and structure.

ACTIVITIES

1. Use characters you developed previously or develop new characters, a protagonist and an antagonist. Now develop an inciting incident that upsets the balance of their lives. You can use any one of the types of opposition discussed in the chapter.

109

2. Outline a series of three or four scenes between the protagonist and the antagonist that logically grows from the inciting incident.

3. Write one of the scenes. You can write the incident as part of a scene, if you wish. Or you can choose a scene that would come later in your play.

4. Determine a logical turning point and climax for the scenes you've been developing to this point.

5. Write a description of the universe, world and time in which this play exists. Go over it to see if you've included everything necessary for the audience to know in order to understand the story.

6. Write a climactic scene for the play you've been developing through the first few questions.

7. Write a new scene in which you show at least one example of each of the three reasons for dramatic action. Remember that the reasons are:

a. to advance the plot.

b. to reveal character.

c. to set the atmosphere.

CHAPTER 7

Dramatic Structure II

Plot can be defined as the revelation of character because it is the narration of how a character acts and reacts when faced with opposition and conflict.

As you know, each character in a play has a goal, which may change direction slightly from scene to scene as the character adapts to new circumstances. However, there is an overall objective, often called the super-objective, each character wants to attain. For instance, in a play I wrote years ago, the central character, Rita, at age thirty-two, still held onto unrealistic dreams of a life of glamour and so was unable to accept an adult role in life. She had always had dreams of bettering herself and of rising above her early environment. Because she saw glamour in a life in the theatre, she held tightly to the idea of becoming an actress. Her dream of adulation and financial success was completely unrealistic, based on the fact that she appeared in a high school play and received the praise of her drama coach and members of the audience.

Rita's father worked sporadically, but was usually too drunk to hold a job. Her mother, a chronic complainer, finally drove her husband into leaving home.

Rita has been married for nearly eighteen years. She and her husband started dating in the tenth grade. Rita was flattered by his attention, and from this involvement she became pregnant.

Rita feels that she missed out on much of the fun and excitement of being young, so aging becomes a serious problem for her. As the years pass, she fails to admit that the possibility of leading a glamorous existence is becoming more remote. So her super objective could be stated as: "Rita wants a life of glamour and adulation." She sees herself achieving this, of course, by becoming a well-known and well-loved actress.

This is on the surface. Underneath, she is a frightened, terribly insecure woman, who desperately needs love and acceptance. Her feelings are intensified by the fact that when the play opens, she and her husband Howie, after years of struggle, finally are out of debt. Now Rita feels she can begin to live. She

starts to spend money wildly, with no thought of the consequences, and to ignore her children. She sees herself as the center of all activity to make up for the fact that to her parents she
felt she didn't matter at all. Underneath the action are the
themes of insecurity and an emotionally underdeveloped little
girl desperately needing her mother and father's love. But the
substitute for this is her dream of being loved by everyone
because of her acting. She simply will not allow herself to consider that her goal is completely unrealistic.

There are several issues at work here. For years, the idea of
her rejection, added to the fact that she had to quit school at fifteen, makes her feel she never had a real chance at life. Instead,
her parents and then her husband Howie dictated how she
should live. So the past rankles, and the catalyst to her change
(or downfall) is that she now has a degree of financial security.
She blows this all out of proportion because she never had any
extra money or often even the basics when she was a child and
a young woman. So she has her past, the forces of suppression
and her family all opposed to what she wants. Of course, now
most of the opposition is only in her mind. But she figures she's
finally going to go after what she wants.

As you might gather, there's a great deal of exposition that
has to be brought out in the play since so much of Rita's present
life depends on what has happened to her in the past. You will
see in Chapter 11 that there are many ways of presenting exposition, but do keep in mind that it should be woven in gradually or the audience won't make the effort to remember it.

ACTION AND SUBPLOTS

There are many ways in which the action in a play can progress,
that is various types of central problems. Just a few of these are:

1. The need for revenge as in *Hamlet*.

2. Being lured by money, sex, fame, *The Tragical History of
Dr. Faustus*.

3. The need to escape an intolerable situation such as family or job,

4. Arriving at a crossroads, and not knowing which way to
turn, being offered two completely different and important
choices.

112

5. Testing others to see how far you can go, both Helen and Annie Sullivan in *The Miracle Worker*.

One way of looking at the action in a play is as a power struggle to see who has the upper hand. This sort of thing is very much apparent in the play *Who's Afraid of Virginia Woolf?* by Edward Albee. First George and then Martha do their best to squelch each other by saying things they know are bound to hurt their spouse.

Many plays have a subplot. An example is in *The Little Foxes*, where Alexandra, Regina's daughter, gradually comes to the realization that she cannot love or even stay with a woman as corrupt or unethical as her mother. And so at the end of the play, although Regina has gained great wealth, she has lost her daughter.

Shakespeare's plays often have subplots, dealing with love affairs or intrigue. For instance, in *As You Like It*, the story that frames the play is that of the wicked Duke Frederick wresting power from his brother, who finds refuge in the Forest of Arden. At the end of the play, the exiled duke is welcomed back. However, the play really is more concerned with the love story of Rosalind and Orlando. There are two further subplots concerned with love stories.

In my play, with the central character of Rita, a subplot deals with her and Howie's two teenagers having, in effect, to become the adults in the family.

A subplot can add depth and interest. Just be certain that you keep the focus on the main action, with the subplot being secondary.

SCENES

Often an act of a play is divided into two or three scenes. These are just arbitrary divisions that have little to do with motivational units or scenes of action. They really are just ways of dividing the play, much as chapters divide a book. Within each chapter can be a lot of different ideas (scenes). A play, for instance, may have Act I, Scene i, occurring on a particular afternoon. Act I, Scene ii, may be that evening.

The type of scenes a playwright should mostly be concerned with are those that begin and end a particular action.

113

There are two ways of defining this sort of scene, although the definitions are similar in that both begin and end with a change in the complications or the crises.

First, a scene can be thought of as a motivational unit, in which the protagonist has a goal he or she has to achieve. Each new scene then occurs when the circumstances change. A character may suddenly be reminded of something which brings about a change, or one character may bring up something new that triggers a different emotional response in another.

For instance, in the following from *NHI: No Human Involved* (the last part of which you already read in Chapter 4), Joe at first is trying to figure out a way to catch the person who has been murdering street people who eat food from city trash bins. So the conflict, though not direct, deals with his trying to figure out how to discover and capture the murderer. Then his motivation or conflict changes somewhat when Nadine says that officially she's not supposed to help him. Perhaps unfairly, he starts to argue, the direction switches somewhat within the following, so that there are really two motivational units — the first to catch the murderer, the second to argue Nadine into helping him.

JOE: So anyhow, I asked around, and nobody seems to know anything. Or else nobody's talking.
NADINE: They don't trust you anymore?
JOE: They trust me. At least most of them. But something's got everyone spooked.
NADINE: The street people?
JOE: Yeah, beyond the usual avoidance of getting involved. Damn, it's so senseless. Who would deliberately set out to kill people by putting poisoned food out in trash cans?
NADINE: The same kind, I suppose, who put razor blades in kids' apples on Halloween.
JOE: When I was a kid, we never locked our doors. Never even thought about it. Parents didn't worry about letting kids play in the park, or around the streetlight on a summer night.
NADINE: You think the perp is some kind of crazy?
JOE: What else?

NADINE: Serial killer?

JOE: There's no pattern, no ritual.

NADINE: Just because something usually happens doesn't mean it always will.

JOE: Yeah, well ...

NADINE: You're not convinced.

JOE: What about you? Any theories?

NADINE: You know I'm not supposed to have theories.

JOE: Is that bitterness I hear?

NADINE: I don't like this any more than you do. But you're in a better position. You were on the force. You know how to handle things. *(Pause)* I sympathize, Joe, and I'll do whatever I can.

JOE: Short of jeopardizing your job.

NADINE: Hey, look, Joe, there are few women who even make sergeant in this town. Let alone lieutenant.

JOE: And you wouldn't want to besmirch your spotless —

Another way of looking at a scene is to say that it begins with the entrance and ends with the exit of an important character. This is called a *French scene*, and it stands to reason that the direction would somewhat change when a major character enters or exits. Throughout the play, Joe also comes into conflict with others: Police Lt. Carl Dombrowski who hates street people; Benjamin, a street person, who feels Joe must have ulterior motives for wanting to find the murderer, and so on. In the following, the conflict and motivation change both with Dombrowski's entrance and his exit. (It also changes, incidentally, when Zippo says Petey is dead.) Zippo, Sadie and Benjamin all are street people. Joe, incidentally, now is a private detective. Previously, he was a policeman, and then due to budget cuts was let go. He spent time on the streets as one of the homeless.

BENJAMIN: *(Sarcastically)* Well, Joe, why don't you tell me what it's like living here on the street? Always wanted to broaden my education. Wanted to understand those poor unfortunates who got no home.

SADIE: What's wrong wit' choo, Benjamin? Why you down on Joe? He be one of us.

BENJAMIN: Yeah. Like an extra hole in the head, like an extra toe on the foot —

115

ZIPPO: Why don't you jes' keep quiet, man? You don't know what you talkin' about.

BENJAMIN: The Lighter Man has spoken.

JOE: You're right, Benjamin, I fell on hard times, but things got better. That doesn't mean I'm going to forget what I had here.

BENJAMIN: Oh, yeah? What was that?

JOE: I like to think I had friends, people I care about. People I don't want to see dying like this.

SADIE: Someone else dead? Who dead now?

ZIPPO: Petey.

SADIE: The one who stay with Maude?

ZIPPO: Yeah.

SADIE: Man, she gonna miss him. I don't know how she gonna get along. *(A car screeches to a halt. A car door slams. Footsteps come closer and stop.)*

ZIPPO: *(Flicking his lighter open and shut)* To what do we owe the pleasure, Officer Dombrowski?

CARL: So, Donaldson, you're sticking your nose in where it don't belong.

JOE: We never got along, Carl, not since the academy. But last time I looked, this was still a free country. I have a right to be with my friends.

CARL: Your friends. *(Mocking laugh)* Figures you'd get excited about a bunch of NHIs.

JOE: Of course, you're better than they are.

CARL: Oh, I know all about your time on the street. Guys used to laugh about it down at the station.

JOE: Guys laugh about it, huh?

CARL: You better believe it. I mean you amongst all them NHIs. You almost became an NHI too.

JOE: I don't suppose anyone's got a lead on the killings.

CARL: A lead? You're kiddin', right? A guy clears the street of rubbish, we're gonna try to stop him? Give me a break.

JOE: That's what these people are to you? Garbage?

ZIPPO: Hey, Joe, whyn't we let Officer Dombrowski go 'bout his duties?

SADIE: Yeah, Joe, what good it be if —

CARL: NHI, no human involved. You hear them, Donaldson? They know what's right.

ZIPPO: Man's jes' doin' his job, Joe.

116

CARL: So what do you say, folks? Can we break up this cozy little get-together?

Within each scene are "beats," points of stress or emphasis, such as occur in poetry or music. With each "beat" the action somehow intensifies but does not really change directions. There is a new beat each time a character gets the upper hand.

Or in the following where Tom has gone to a bar to get his nephew, who is underage. (Robbie, Phil and Saul are customers.)

Beat One:

ROBBIE: *(sitting at a table with PHIL and SAUL)* Why don't you leave him alone? Pick on someone your own size.
TOM: It's not your concern.
ROBBIE: Yeah, well, I'm making it my concern.
TOM: *(turning to BILLY)* Do you know this guy? *(ROBBIE jumps up and swings at TOM, grazing his chin.)*
TOM: Come on, damn it. He's my nephew, and he's only seventeen!

Here the action intensifies when the two other men become actively involved, so we have Beat Two.

(PHIL and SAUL jump up. ALL THREE MEN surround TOM.)
SAUL: Robbie has it right. Why don't you just get lost?
ROBBIE: And like I said, leave this man alone!

A general rule is that there usually are less complications in a tragedy than in a comedy, but they are more serious in nature. Comedy often contains a great many reversals and complications, though many are superficial. The unexpected provides the humor, and the audience doesn't identify so strongly with the characters.

SELECTIVITY

To maintain interest and avoid confusion, the action of a play has to be condensed. Much of life is mundane, with little of interest occurring. So a play has to be selective to maintain an audience's interest. An action that would take longer in life is compressed and heightened in a play. Dialog is more purposeful; inconsequential activity is eliminated. Sometimes two things

117

that take place separately in normal life can be combined — having to deal with two crises or separate situations at once. Often several events are occurring at the same time. For instance, the love stories are taking place in *As You Like It* while the Duke is holding court in the forest, hoping to regain his land and title.

Time is condensed. Things are accomplished more quickly and sentences formulated into a better structure on the stage, while still appearing or sounding natural. It would be rare indeed in real life to find any two people who have such a command of their language and thoughts under intense emotion as do George and Martha in *Who's Afraid of Virginia Woolf?* In the following chapters on dialog and characterization, there will be a further discussion of selectivity as a way to maintain an audience's interest.

More than this, however, you usually can think of a play in terms of an analogy. The actions are universal; they relate to all (or most) of us, or we would not be interested. Although they deal with specific characters doing specific things, they stand for something larger.

NHI: No Human Involved is about the little guy versus overwhelming bureaucracy. Its theme might be: that "You can fight city hall and win." It's about people with little hope triumphing. *The Little Foxes* is about overwhelming greed, which destroys everything else in life.

In plays, as in life, people speak through implication and draw conclusions through inference. Most of the time, they do not come out and say exactly what they mean. The following scene is from *Goat Song* by Franz Werfel. The play takes place at the close of the eighteenth century. The parents of Stanja, betrothed to Mirko, have just dropped her off so she will get used to his farm. In the following, what Mirko really is saying is that he does not understand Stanja and because of this he is becoming very frustrated with her, so frustrated that he says he will beat her after they are married.

MIRKO: Your parents are gone now. Are you sad?
STANJA: No, I am not sad.
MIRKO: Then you don't love your parents?
STANJA: I love them.

MIRKO: Then you must be sad. Doesn't it hurt you when something is over? The axle creaks, the horses draw up, the whip.... And then, something is ended.

STANJA: I never ache for what is past.

MIRKO: Oh, I often do. I can lie in the meadow hour after hour longing for the games I played there on the grass.

STANJA: That is because you are a man. *(Short pause)*

MIRKO: Do the house and the farm please you?

STANJA: Why shouldn't they? House, rooms, chimneys, stables, pigsties, and hencoops and dovecotes, same as everywhere.

MIRKO: And do I please you?

STANJA: Why shouldn't you please me?

MIRKO: Do you know, Stanja, I would have liked it better if you had cried before, when they left you.... *(Suddenly turns on her)* You! What if you've loved someone before! Tell me! Have you loved someone else?

STANJA *(Hesitatingly)*: No.

MIRKO *(Slowly, his eyes closed)*: I think, when we're married, I will beat you.

STANJA: That's what all husbands do.

A playwright rarely spells everything out, even in the conclusions. In the ending of Elizabeth Wong's *Letters to a Student Revolutionary*, we never discover for certain that Karen, the Chinese woman who participated in the Tiananmen Square revolt in which hundreds of students were massacred, dies or not. The playwright never comes out and says that the situation was an atrocity, though this is what she meant.

OTHER TYPES OF STRUCTURES

Although the story play is the most common, there are several other ways of structuring a play. One is thematic structure. There may be a variety of scenes all dealing with the same basic issues but unrelated to each other in continuity or in characterization.

This is the sort of structure I'm using in my play *One Moment in Time*, which portrays four sets of murderer/victims. Although the characters do not even know each other, they are tied together by the "roles" they play.

119

The type of play that relies on theme for unity often is episodic; it does not build toward a single turning point and climax. Such is the case with the four sets of murderers and victims. The play will focus for a time on one set before flashing to another. Occasionally, two or three sets of characters will appear, each in different areas of the stage.

Although the play, as such, has no overall plot, within each "story," each specific tale of murder, there will be an inciting incident that leads to the climax (or murder) and falling action to show the results of what happened to the killers.

Another type of structure is circular, where the plays start out one way and end with the same set of circumstances. These plays usually also are thematic, so that there are two types of structure melded together. Absurdist plays usually are like this. A good example is Ionesco's *The Bald Soprano*, where the action begins and ends in the same way. There is a single set of characters, who sometimes shout at each other, but we as the audience do not know why because the language they use is nonsensical. So although there is the appearance of struggle and conflict, the play does not progress toward a resolution.

Another example is *Waiting for Godot*, because things are the same at the end as at the beginning.

A play may be presented just to portray a facet of life or a way of life. One that has strong characterizations but no real cause-to-effect plot is Paul Zindel's *The Effects of Gamma Rays on Man in the Moon Marigolds*. It deals with the relationships among a mother and two daughters. Another example, though it does have somewhat of a plot, is *Torch Song Trilogy*, loosely connected one-acts (more unified in the film version) that explore a certain type of gay experience in New York a few decades past.

Sometimes plays without a plot show incidents following each other in chronological order but not necessarily growing out of the preceding material. In this way they differ from the story play. Historical or biographical plays often are like this, and so too can be plays that are tied to a certain occurrence such as a trial. When the trial ends, so does the play. Such plays also may have a plot, but this is not always true.

ACTIVITIES

1. Can you think of other types of conflict a play can deal with besides those listed (like the need for revenge, the need to escape and so on)?

2. Do you think the play you are writing would benefit from developing a subplot? Why?

3. Write a scene, whether for your play or not, that has at least two beats.

4. Write a French scene clearly showing a change to a new motivational unit with the entrance or exit of a character.

CHAPTER 8

Audience and Theme

Before you start to develop a complete play, there are two things you should think about. Why do you want to write it? What audience do you want to reach? The two, of course, are tied closely together.

CHOOSING YOUR AUDIENCE

Except maybe when you're learning the rules of playwriting, there's no good reason for writing a play without an audience in mind. It's fine to write isolated scenes and monologs and bits of dialog, which can help you focus better or give you ideas for plays, but you need to focus on a particular goal to get anywhere with writing or anything else.

So it's a good idea to give some thought to the type of audience you want to reach and why. If you're not sure, maybe it will help to begin by asking yourself some general questions about your writing:

1. What sort of play do I like?

If you're thinking about a particular subject or approach, take this into consideration. If someone else were writing a play on the same subject, would you want to see it? Why?

2. Will the subjects that interest me, interest others?

The following actually happened to me today:

DENTIST: I had a girlfriend who was a newspaper reporter. She said you could always tell who the single reporters were dating.
ME: Oh, yeah? Why's that?
DENTIST: The stories they wrote about them, stories nobody else in the world would be interested in. "Why I Chose Pedicuring Dogs as a Profession."

On the other hand, don't eliminate a subject or approach just because the theme or subject matter is limited. Remember that plays are analogies, symbols for something larger. Though your subject matter may be entomology, you can give the play a broad appeal by showing human emotions and needs related to the subject.

For example, an entomologist discovers a new species of insect but someone else claims to have discovered it first.

3. What is your purpose in wanting to write plays?

Over the past few decades, Neil Simon has often been criticized for the type of plays he writes. Critics accuse him of being a lightweight, of not saying anything important in his comedies. Yet he is probably the most popular contemporary playwright. Such hits as *California Suite*, *The Sunshine Boys*, *Barefoot in the Park*, and *The Odd Couple* fulfill the audience's need for escapism, proving he's defined his reasons for writing, and he knows his audience.

Of course, Simon is not writing for the same audience as Wendy Kesselman, who, for instance, wrote *My Sister in This House* after reading about a murder case in 1933 where two sisters, Christine and Lea Papin, murdered the mistress and daughter of the house where they worked in Paris.

TYPES OF AUDIENCES

Although the divisions are not clear-cut and there's a lot of overlapping among types of audience, people attend the theatre for three major reasons: first and most important, to be entertained; second, to gain insight into their own lives, and third, to learn.

ARTS REPORTER: So here we are at the opening of what certainly will prove to be another successful production for America's best-loved playwright, Stu Dent. It's intermission time, and the lobby is abuzz with laughter and conversation. Let's see if we can talk to a few theatergoers here to see their reactions, and what they expect from Mr. Dent's plays. Sir, oh, sir?

SIR: You talkin' ta me?

ARTS REPORTER: I'd like to have your reaction to Mr. Dent's new drama and whether you've seen his previous hits.

SIR: Oh, yeah, I've been here for every one of 'em.

ARTS REPORTER: Interesting. Now I want to ask you. As you may know, people attend the theatre for a variety of reasons. Entertainment, enlightenment.

SIR: The food.

ARTS REPORTER: I'm sorry?

124

SIR: The food at the opening night reception. Best in town. Been coming to opening nights here for years. None of those silly little sandwiches about as big as a two-bit piece. No, sir, here they have a sandwich that's a sandwich. And the champagne —

ARTS REPORTER: Are you serious?

SIR: Of course.

ARTS REPORTER: But the play. What did you think of the play?

SIR: Aw, who needs it. See this? The latest Clancy novel. I sit and read it till it's time to eat. Uh, excuse me, but I see they're setting up early. Maybe I can grab me a sandwich and ...

Most audiences want to get away from everyday monotony and problems. They like comedies, thrillers and musicals. People who want to learn something or have their own beliefs reinforced are more likely to attend plays dealing with serious subject matter. Finally, those who view theatre largely as an art form probably would choose to view period plays or experimental theatre.

Each audience member may attend a play for a combination of reasons, or see different plays for different reasons. Each may attend a variety of theatres: educational, community and professional.

Generally, college or university theatre exists for teaching, both those involved in the production and audience members. Therefore, there will be a wide variety of genres and styles. Elementary, junior high and high school theatre most often exist for fun, although many of them also have courses in various facets of theatre.

Community theatres exist largely for entertainment, though some present experimental plays. Professional theatre exists to make money for the producers. Broadway theatre is much different from off-Broadway and off-off-Broadway. The former stays with more traditional drama, while the latter is open to more experimentation, although in recent years off-Broadway also is becoming more reluctant to take chances.

Even though professional theatre exists to make money, some commercial theatres encourage writing by newcomers.

125

Because they exist mainly to give pleasure to as many people as possible, community theatres will produce plays that the members believe will be enjoyed. Often this is an excellent starting place for a new playwright since many of them actively seek submissions. You have a better chance of having your script accepted if you know the area and the type of people who attend plays there. A community theatre is more willing to take a chance on an inexperienced writer than is a Broadway theatre since there's not nearly so much money to be lost if the play isn't well-received.

College and university theatres also offer a better chance of production to the beginning playwright than does professional theatre. Educational theatre for the most part exists as a training ground. It can serve this function for the writer as well as the directors, designers, actors, technicians and audiences. Even if you cannot have your work produced as one of the school's major offerings, you often have the opportunity for workshop productions. Most schools have experimental theatres in which you are free to do as you choose with little restriction, and most accept work from outsiders as well as students. Of course, you should know the type of school, if not the specific school, for which you are writing. Some plays that might be acceptable at a large state university, for instance, would be rejected at a small, church-related college.

The type of play that can be done by an academic, a professional or a community theatre in one area may not be acceptable somewhere else. What draws audiences in New York City may leave a lot of empty seats in Zanesville, Ohio. The moral outlook and general attitudes differ from area to area. A large city has more types of people from which to draw than does a small community.

If you are from New Jersey or Maine, it would be presumptuous to attempt to write a play specifically for a Midwestern audience, unless you've lived in the Midwest for a number of years. The point is you need to investigate and/or know about the audience and theatres for which you hope to write.

It really isn't difficult to have a good play produced. A few years ago I asked members of a playwriting workshop I conducted to see how many of the thirty-some professional and community theatres in the San Diego area would accept original scripts. Surprisingly, every one of them said they would at least be willing to look at them. One or two, e.g., the Old Globe, now require submissions by agents, but they still do consider original scripts.

GAINING AUDIENCE INTEREST

Suppose you've investigated various theatres for which you want to write and have thought through your ideas. How do you interest the audience in what you have to say? How do you handle the subject matter?

It depends a lot on your purpose in writing. Playwrights often attempt to reinforce a common belief as Thornton Wilder did in *Our Town*. The play states very strongly that we should learn to pay attention to each other and make the most of our lives and our relationships. There is certainly nothing new in this idea, but Wilder states it poignantly and well, as evidenced by its continuing popularity in all types of theatres from high school to professional.

Lorraine Hansberry's *A Raisin in the Sun* is a powerful play because it also deals with a common theme. One of the characters, Walter Younger, a black man, finally recognizes that true success in life can never come through compromising yourself and your personal dignity. All his life he's defined success as being synonymous with money. Then he's forced to choose between accepting a large amount of cash not to move into a white neighborhood or refusing it and retaining his self-respect.

A writer may deal with something relatively alien to the experience of the audience. Then maybe the goal is one of enlightenment. Historical plays often fall into this category, though many that do so have other themes as well. Peter Shaffer's *The Royal Hunt of the Sun*, for example, is set in the framework of Pizarro's conquest of the Incas in Peru. But it is also centered around a theme of lost faith. Cizmar's *The Death of a Miner* is alien to most people in its story about coal miners in West Virginia, but, of course, its concern with human rights is not at all alien, nor is Elizabeth Wong's play *Letters to a Student Revolutionary*, even though it deals with the massacre of Chinese students by a government that allows no freedom of choice or expression. Although most of us have not lived in China, we can empathize with the theme of suppression.

127

Even though the situations and characters are strange or different, they have to have elements with which the audience can identify. A play must deal with human emotions and problems, even if the central characters are Martians or Venusians. Otherwise, the play will have little meaning for the spectators. Audience members most often want to identify with and care about the central character.

On the other hand, Berthold Brecht is highly regarded for his Theatre of Alienation in which the ideas and situations are more important than the characters. When Brecht rehearsed his plays, he sometimes had the actors add, "he said," or "she said," after each line because he wanted them to remain emotionally detached from their roles. Often his characters appeared for only a limited time in an attempt to prevent audience involvement. In such plays as *Mother Courage and Her Children*, Brecht emphasized social or political problems more than characterization, yet managed to express strong sympathy for the human condition. Even in Absurdist drama the human condition rather than the individual characters is important, since the characters often exhibit traits of automatism and speak with illogical or disjointed dialog.

To George Bernard Shaw, ideas also were often more important than characters, who sometimes carried on long conversations on philosophy and religion. An example is the "Don Juan in Hell" scene from *Man and Superman*.

Any presentation, whether it's a speech, an interpretive reading or a short story, has a better chance of success if it's written with a specific audience in mind. In other words, no matter what you write, other than private thoughts, you will have little chance of success if you don't constantly think of this audience.

For instance, I would never consider submitting an adaptation of *One Moment in Time* to the producer for whom I write experimental audio plays, nor would I submit *To Ride a Wild Pony*, which deals with the theme of financial dependence, to a publisher who targets mostly high schools.

REACHING YOUR AUDIENCE

When analyzing audiences, you need to take into consideration such things as background, political leanings, social and economic circumstances, general views of life and geographic locations.

PLAYWRIGHT: Mind if I ask you something?
MAN-ON-THE-STREET: Yeah, what?
PLAYWRIGHT: Do you ever attend the theatre?
MAN: Sometimes, why?
PLAYWRIGHT: Well then, are you a right winger, left winger, middle of —
MAN: What has that got —
PLAYWRIGHT: Where'd you grow up? Did you go to college? What do you do? How much money do you make?
MAN: Now just wait one minute!
PLAYWRIGHT: Well, you see, I'm thinking of writing this play, and I want to find out as much as I can —
MAN: Play, you're writing a play.
PLAYWRIGHT: Well, yeah.
MAN: Oh, well then. *(Assuming a theatrical pose and voice)* O, pardon me, thou bleeding piece of earth, that I am meek and gentle with these butchers. Thou art the ruins of the noblest man — *(His own voice)* I'm an actor. Unemployed actor. Unemployed for years. Waiting for my break. My big break. God, I'd give anything —
PLAYWRIGHT: Uh, yeah, well, thank you, sir.

Almost any idea, if it's universal (that is, if it has meaning for most people) can be the basis for a play. The manner in which it is presented — the characters, the setting, the dialog and the situations — determines whether it will hold an audience's attention. The musical *Godspell*, through its characters, situations and music, obviously appealed to a younger audience than did *Evita*, even though both had successful runs in New York a number of years back. The former takes place on a playground and has a group of young people who enact Christ's parables and episodes from His life, as taken from the book of "Matthew." *Evita* is a biographical opera about the life of Eva Peron, who rose to power in the 1940s in Argentina.

A story or play has to progress logically with the characters attempting to solve their own problems. Except if it's a spoof, it's unlikely that any drama in which coincidence plays a major part will attract a large audience. The central character either triumphs or falls to defeat on his or her own merits. Early

129

events should sow the seeds for the turning point or climax. The detective attempts to discover who committed the murder. As a member of the audience, you know it is someone who has been introduced early on in the action. Any characters who play important roles in the outcome must be introduced early, either through actual appearance or through reference. It would be illogical if they were not.

In real life it's different. Police looking for a murderer may have no idea of the motive for the crime nor of the type of person they are seeking. Yet, crimes are solved.

THEME

Theme is the central message of the play; it is what a playwright wants to say to an audience, and so is tied closely to audience response. How does the playwright want the audience to feel after the final curtain? Why? Maybe the writer wants only to call attention to something important or worth remembering, point up a social problem or look more closely at their own values.

STUDENT: Theme? Theme? I have to write a theme. Wow, you know, I haven't written a theme since high school English. I mean, hey, man, I thought this was a playwriting class. And you're asking me to do a theme.

PROFESSOR: Mom always told me I should be a plumber.

The audience will be more willing to accept the message of the play if they are in at least partial agreement with it. This means you have a better chance of reaching the audience by beginning with a common premise, something the audience members already believe, e.g., that war is wrong, and then building upon it.

Often, theme is simply an observation of life, rather than a concrete statement. The Absurdist dramatists, for example, state that life is absurd without trying to urge any point of view upon the audience. The audience is expected to draw their own conclusions.

If you start with a character, you may find that what he or she says and does determines the theme. On the other hand, you may start out by wanting to make a particular statement.

If you do, be careful that characters don't become merely mouthpieces and not real people and that the writing doesn't become too rigid. An example of this type of writing is the thesis drama developed by such men as Alexander Dumas, fils, who wrote *Camille*. The aim was to teach a lesson or to correct a moral wrong. The stage became a pulpit. In fairness, thesis play can be a strong form, as evidenced in some of the plays of Henrik Ibsen.

DEVELOPING SUBJECT MATTER AND THEME

When it comes to writing, each of us has two advantages, although they may seem to contradict each other. One is that our backgrounds and experiences are different; the other is that they are similar.

To appeal to an audience, a play must have elements which are recognizable. There has to be a common ground upon which the audience and the playwright meet. Even if you live in California, you have much in common with a person who lives in Rhode Island. American citizens experience emotions similar to those felt by Chilean citizens. No human being is totally alien to any other human being. We all experience the same sort of feelings, and we've all been in similar situations. Every emotion that can be felt by a human being certainly has been felt.

Psychologists say that human beings learn by relating new situations and encounters to what they already know. They build upon previous knowledge and in this way expand their universe. Audiences relate the action onstage to their own backgrounds and personalities. Both theatre and life are related to humankind's mimetic instinct. But there would be no such thing as imitation if there were no need to relate other's actions to our own lives. We do all share common experiences and common goals.

Conversely, the chain of events that makes up your life differs from that of anybody else. Your perceptions of the world and your interpretation of events are slightly different in some cases and vastly different in others to anyone else's views of the same things. That accounts in part for the difficulty policemen often have in obtaining a description of a robber. Each witness describes the person differently. Our mental attitudes color our perceptions.

131

In one of the stories in *Welcome to the Monkey House*, Kurt Vonnegut, Jr., writes about a society in which there were attempts to make everyone equal by handicapping those individuals who had outstanding abilities or attributes in any one area. The handsome or beautiful were masked; the intelligent had their thoughts interrupted electronically, and the physically strong had to carry added weight. The idea of such a society appears ridiculous to us. We need a sense of personal identity.

When choosing ideas for a play, you need a balance between what is common to everyone in the audience and what is unique to the individual.

The individuality of your background and perceptions will hold an audience's attention while at the same time you are making a common or universal statement.

You have experienced childhood and have grown through adolescence to adulthood. If you had the time and the inclination, you could write literally dozens of plays about growing up.

You could deal with specifics or present an eclectic view of your childhood and adolescence. You could try to recapture a particular period as was done by the authors of the musical, *Grease*, which did little more than present a facet of teenage life in the fifties. Compare the musical *Annie*, based on the comic strip, *Little Orphan Annie*, with *The Miracle Worker* or *The Diary of Anne Frank*. *The Miracle Worker* is much more specific in its focus on the relationship between Helen Keller and her teacher, Annie Sullivan, and so is *The Diary of Anne Frank*, based on a journal written by a teenager forced to hide in an Amsterdam attic to escape the Nazis.

Your views of childhood may differ a lot from these. But what might you want to say about your early years? Start with an examination of your attitudes. Do you view your childhood with nostalgia? Are you resentful about the way you were treated by your parents? What provided the highlights or the biggest disappointments?

You have only to look around you for all sorts of ideas. Look at people, events, institutions or attitudes, but examine them critically. Learn to analyze how you feel about the things you encounter in everyday life. Part of the success in writing is living up to the old maxim: "Know thyself." As Jean and Veryl

Rosenbaum state in *The Writer's Survival Guide* (Writer's Digest Books), you should examine your psychohistory as a means of knowing self and then being able to use this knowledge in writing. This means asking yourself questions similar to those you asked when developing a character. As the Rosenbaums state: "You will discover a more spontaneous recall if you respond to the questions with feelings rather than intellect." You begin asking yourself questions about your earliest childhood and advance through life. This sort of thing helps you know and often understand your feelings and thus provides you with material for writing.

SELF-ANALYST: *(Sitting in desk chair, knees crossed, steno pad resting on one knee, pen poised above it)* **So, what is your very first memory, me?**

SELF-ANALYST: *(Rushing to black leather couch, lying down, hands at side)* **Well, let's see now. It was dark, really dark. And I was all wet.**

SELF-ANALYST: *(Rushing back to the desk chair and sitting)* **Dark, wet? When was that? How old were you?**

SELF-ANALYST: *(Hurrying back to couch and lying down)* **Old? I wasn't old. I wasn't even born yet!**

Once you learn to examine and evaluate your own life, you will have a better idea of what you can write. Your approach or the way you feel will determine the kind of play. Is there something you want to ridicule? Or should the same subject be treated in a light, humorous vein? Perhaps it demands a serious treatment. No matter what ideas or opinions you have, you can treat them in any number of ways.

Many writers have examined the social environment of their time and come up with a play, whether the purpose was to call attention to something or to make fun of it. Such diverse presentations resulted in Gilbert and Sullivan's satire of the British navy in *HMS Pinafore* and Ibsen's dramatizations of women's oppression in *Ghosts*.

OUR BASIC NEEDS

Another way of choosing a subject or theme for a play is to examine basic needs, those things that are necessary to sustain a reasonably happy life. Basic needs include such things as secu-

133

rity, recognition, response, adventure, worship and self-preservation. Each of these can be broken down into many sub-classifications. For instance, what types of security do people need? We need physical security. We want the law to protect us. We want to feel secure in knowing that if we step outside we won't be mugged. We want financial security. We need money for food, clothing and shelter, all basic necessities. We want to feel comfortable in social situations, and the security of good health. The list is almost endless.

Take one of these types of security and look at how it can be treated in a play, governmental security, for instance, which would include themes about war and peace. They range from *What Price Glory?* to *Arms and the Man*. The former, a comedy about World War I by Laurence Stallings and Maxwell Anderson, was outspoken in its dialog and authentic treatment of war. Writer and drama professor John Gassner says it did more than any other play to promote the cause of realism and freedom of speech on the American stage. Shaw's *Arms and the Man*, a satire on soldiering, war and romantic melodrama, contains such characters as Captain Bluntschli who carries chocolates in his cartridge belt and a heroine who is an unconscionable liar.

Another need is for recognition. A person wants status, which can range from recognition of musical ability to success in business. Consider the person who heads community fund drives. This person may believe in the causes but may be for the most part motivated by being praised for being so unselfish.

STUDENT: But I need a car, Dad. All my friends have cars. If I don't have one, it's going to affect my entire life. I need to feel comfortable socially; I need acceptance by my peer group. You wouldn't want me to go through life feeling rejected and socially inferior, would you, Dad?

DAD: Well, son, look at it this way. You need to feel accepted socially. I need to have financial security. Buying you a car is not the way for me to have financial security.

STUDENT: Daaaad!

DAD: Okay, I'll make you a deal. I'll use your mom's and my savings and buy you a car. A good car. One that will make you the envy of all of your friends.

STUDENT: Recognition! Yes, Dad, yes, that's important too.

DAD: And you will respect me then, my boy. Respect me so much that you will do anything in your power to please me. You will drive me to work every day in your wonderful car. You will pick me up. You will take me to meetings and conferences, to my bowling league, because you will respect me deeply.

STUDENT: But Dad —

DAD: Are you rejecting me, son?

STUDENT: Dad, you can't be serious!

DAD: Will I never again be able to hold my head up high? Will I slink through the office, through social obligations, eyes averted, hoping no one asks me the dreaded question: How is your son? But if they do, I'll say, "Oh, my son is fine. He's doing so well with his new car. He's the envy of all his friends." But my voice will be sad, son; it will have no wit, no sparkle. And then my friends will feel sorry for me, at least to my face. Behind my back, they'll snicker and gossip. "What do you think of old Art Crenshaw?" they'll ask. "No one respects him; he must be pretty worthless." And I'll be rejected, and —

STUDENT: Well then, Dad — could you maybe help me buy a second-hand bike?

DAD: Of course, son. Whatever you want. Nothing's too good for my boy.

Simply thinking about what needs you have and how you would react if any of them are taken away, can give you many ideas for your writing.

WRITE ABOUT WHAT YOU KNOW

Ideas are all around you, and almost anything can start you thinking about a play you can write: a conversation you overhear, the way someone walks down the street, a particular location.

Ideas can come from a situation, a bit of dialog or a character. But it's good to heed the old advice: "Write what you know." Stay within your own experience. What does this mean? Does it mean that if you have never been an uncle, you cannot write about uncles, or if you have never been a basketball player you cannot write about basketball players? Does it mean if you are a man you cannot write a play whose central character is a woman? Of course not. If you were limited to what you have experienced personally, you could have only one character, or at most several variations of one character in every play.

Rather than just writing about what you've experienced, include things you've observed as well. But be sure you know enough about them to be convincing. If you've never visited France, it would be foolish to write a play that takes place in Paris. If your setting is New England in winter and you have never lived through a winter there, you might not be convincing or credible.

There are exceptions. If the setting is nonrealistic, then you are free to invent. Nobody can say any better than James Hilton what Shangri-la is like. Moss Hart remarked in his autobiography, *Act One,* that he deliberately chose settings that were unfamiliar to him because then he could be more imaginative. But if you do this, you might have some glaring inconsistencies. Sometimes research can make a play seem authentic. One example is historical plays, where it's impossible to observe conditions first-hand.

The Pulitzer Prize-winning playwright Paul Green relied largely upon research in writing his outdoor drama, *Trumpet in the Land*, first produced in 1970 and at this writing, still going strong. The play takes place during the late eighteenth century, so Green couldn't know first-hand about the situations and conditions of the time. But not only did he do research on the period, but he spent a great deal of time in Tuscarawas County, Ohio, where most of the action occurs.

Be sure to check out everything of a factual nature before including it in a play. You cannot change laws or misquote facts to suit your purpose. In the framework of your play you can establish circumstances where facts can be distorted, but the audience must recognize it as such. If you're unsure of your facts, either look them up or don't include them. If you're doing a historical play, begin with research. If you're writing about a particular area or a particular group of people, learn about them.

DETERMINING THEME THROUGH SELECTIVITY

Any time you write you are interpreting life because your

perspective is different from anyone else's. Even histories and supposedly objective news reports are not entirely objective because, of necessity, they cannot contain everything. Reporters include only what — if they are ethical — they consider most important, without attempting to distort views.

Yet any event will be distorted by the writer. That's why, for instance, two old junior high textbooks covering the same period have such names as *The American Civil War* and *The War of Northern Aggression.*

Dramatists, through selectivity, emphasize or focus on what they consider to be important, what matters to them. They exaggerate; they ignore other viewpoints by condensing time and action, by emphasizing character traits and by editing dialog. There's nothing wrong with this; it's what human beings do all the time.

At the beginning of the naturalistic movement, writers, influenced largely by Emile Zola, felt that a play should be only an observation of life. A playwright's job was to record faithfully all details of action, character and setting. There were to be no climaxes, and nothing should be emphasized more than anything else. To plan a beginning or an ending was not being truthful since life is continual. Furthermore, the writer was to include everything he or she observed.

Such a "slice of life" drama had no real theme. It could say nothing to an audience except that "this is a segment of one type of life." Today's audience would find such a form, if presented regularly, boring and monotonous. To test this, go to a party some time and try to record the conversation for two hours without saying anything yourself. You'll probably wonder how the guests can enjoy themselves.

As a playwright, you have to interpret and select. Even if you allow your characters to take the action of the play into their own hands, your mind will blot out much of the inconsequential detail before it reaches the paper. More than that, you can revise, change and heighten during the second or third drafts.

GENRE

Once you decide on an approach, unless you plan to go back and rewrite the entire play, you need to be consistent throughout, or you will confuse and frustrate an audience.

If a play starts out with the audience laughing at a particular character, who then is brutally murdered, the play most likely will be a failure. The treatment has to be consistent, within the play's framework. It has to suit the plot and the characters. We know because of the type character he is that Oedipus in Sophocles' *Oedipus Rex* will continue on until he proves definitely who is the murderer of Laius.

This means that a play should fit a particular genre, or at least have elements of several genres that are not so diverse from each other as to be confusing. For instance, it probably wouldn't work to mix elements of tragedy and farce in a single play, unless you are writing a spoof.

Yet despite my saying this, it is difficult to categorize all plays since many have a strong overlapping and a mixture of various elements. Some plays that are comedies have tragic elements, and tragedies that contain elements of comedy. If we take the oldest definition of tragedy as a form that "shows noble actions of noble men," we have few modern tragedies. In Tennessee Williams' *The Glass Menagerie*, the four characters are trapped by circumstances and their own limitations. The audience feels compassion for them, but there is no point of defeat in the play, so it cannot be classified as a tragedy using most definitions. The defeat has started long before the play opens.

Genre refers to the way playwrights treat their subject matter. The treatment is related to their outlook, at least at a particular time and with a particular subject. The treatment is tied in with the purpose in writing the play. Purpose, of course, is tied closely to theme.

Overall, there are two methods of treating subject matter, serious and comic.

It's impossible to consider genre without considering *style*. Here also are two broad categories, the representational and the presentational.

In the broadest sense, representation tries to convince an audience that what is occurring on stage is like or similar to life. This style then contributes to empathy. We identify with a character whom we feel is like us.

The presentational style, which makes no pretense of life, contributes to aesthetic distance. Here, in extreme examples, there is no attempt to convince the audience that life is taking place on stage. Rather, the style proclaims that theatre simply comes from life.

An audience can be reached by making them feel what the character is feeling. And a play that leans heavily in this direction is serious in nature; it's representational.

On the other hand, comedy is funny because of aesthetic distance. In real life, a man's tripping over a rock and breaking a leg wouldn't be funny. In a comedy it could be. This is because we don't closely identify with the leading characters in most comedies. We keep our aesthetic distance.

There are serious plays, however, like *In White America*, which are largely presentational in that in many of the scenes the actors directly address the audience.

Most plays are neither pure presentation nor pure representation but a mixture. We can identify with the characters in a play and feel their emotions, while at the same time we have no urge to run up onto the stage to help them out of difficulties.

There is no real separation of the two concepts, but if we empathize too much, we lose our objectivity. We become too involved. If we don't identify enough, the play has no meaning.

Tragedy

The most serious genre and so the most representational is tragedy where the playwright asks the audience to identify completely with the protagonist who, after struggling against overwhelming odds, is defeated.

Tragedy deals with serious and profound problems, often with human nature at its most basic, the struggle between good and evil. Tragic protagonists either battle a flaw in themselves, evil in others or conditions.

Hamlet battles against the evil he sees perpetrated by his uncle. Romeo and Juliet battle against a way of life in which two families are feuding. Oedipus and Willy Loman battle against parts of themselves.

The forces opposing the tragic hero are always more powerful than the protagonists. But through defeat they remain

139

noble and in this respect are triumphant.

Tragedy's purpose is to make us experience emotions by identifying with the tragic hero and to reaffirm our faith in ourselves as part of the human race. Even when tragic characters die, their heroism lives. Not their deaths but what the playwright says about life is important. Tragic heroes face the consequences of their actions and realize that they will be defeated. But along the way they experience new insights into themselves.

Comedy

The opposite of tragedy is comedy; its purpose is to make us laugh, most often at ourselves and at our social institutions so that we'll take them less seriously. Molière laughs at hypochondria in *The Imaginary Invalid*. Neil Simon, in *The Odd Couple*, pokes fun at two guys who escape their marriages only to find that they have the same sorts of problems in trying to live with a friend.

Comedy has the greatest variety of any genre of drama. It can be slapstick or gentle. Usually, it shows a deviation from the norm of everyday life, even though it often uses the pettiness of day-to-day living as its subject matter.

There are various reasons for writing comedy. Often it is so that we take ourselves less seriously. Sometimes it's to remind us of our own frailties, but to say they aren't so serious as we sometimes think. A playwright may want to correct social injustice. An excellent example, first produced in 1909, is *How the Vote Was Won*. Written by Cicely Hamilton and Christopher St. John, the play was intended both as a comedy and as propaganda to secure voting rights for women in England. It showed what would happen if all the women in the country stopped working and went to live with their nearest male relative, allowing him to support her.

The idea is that if we can laugh at something that's wrong with society, maybe then we will be more willing to correct it. In other words, comedy should help keep us from gaining too high an opinion of ourselves.

The humor in a comedy can come from character or situations. Any subject matter can be used if it can be treated in a humorous light. It would be cruel, for instance — even though it's been done on such television shows as *Saturday Night Live* —

140

to treat physical deformities or handicaps as sources of comedy.

Such things as eccentricities of character can be humorous, as is Molière's treatment of Harpagon's greed in *The Miser*.

The central characters may become involved in situations outside their knowledge and experience, thus making fun of our tendency to place too much importance on our involvements and our goals.

Unlike tragedy, comedy always ends happily. If the protagonist were to be defeated, the audience would feel guilty for having laughed at him or her. This means that it's important to establish a comic frame of reference so the audience knows either that they aren't to empathize too strongly with any of the characters, or else that it's a matter of laughing with instead of at the protagonist.

There are certain devices you can use to establish a comic frame of reference. They are *derision, incongruity, exaggeration, repetition, surprise* and *character inconsistency*.

Derision means poking fun at people or social institutions in order to bring about change. Just be careful this doesn't become bitter or cruel, or the audience is likely to identify with the intended victim.

Incongruity involves opposites or elements that don't seem to fit together. An example is a tall woman with a short man.

Exaggeration means enlarging something by overstating it. For instance, people aren't really as greedy as Molière's character of Harpagon in *The Miser*. Exaggeration often encompasses the other comic devices by heightening them.

Repetition includes verbal or visual gags done over and over again. An example is a man's tripping over a stool each time he enters or exits. This can be heightened further by bringing in variations. For instance, on one entrance the man is very careful to avoid the stool. Someone calls to him. He starts toward them, ignoring the stool, and trips over it.

Surprise is simply the unexpected. We know every joke will have a punch line. But even though we know it's coming, it's unexpected in what it contains. Surprise includes puns, insults and other verbal wit.

Character inconsistency shows a personality trait that doesn't seem to fit with the others. An example is the kind old

141

ladies who murder old men in Kesselring's *Arsenic and Old Lace.*

Closely related to derision and yet sometimes considered a sub-genre of comedy is satire, which ridicules for the purpose of reform but is gentler.

Melodrama

Another genre is melodrama, which combines elements of comedy and tragedy. It's similar to comedy in that it usually has a happy ending. But it's also related to tragedy because it has a serious subject matter, and the audience identifies or empathizes with the characters. Unlike tragic characters, however, those in melodrama are nearly always one-dimensional or at best less developed.

Melodrama often relies on coincidence or fate. Good always triumphs. The form includes sentimentality. It is often episodic in that only the most exciting events and situations are included. There also is comic relief in the form of the minor characters.

Most of television's so-called dramatic series are melodramas, even though we often do learn to know the continuing protagonists — the detectives or policemen, for instance.

Farce

A fourth genre is farce, similar to melodrama in that fate often plays a part in the outcome. But it's more closely related to comedy. It uses stock characters with no depth, and the plots, highly contrived, rely on physical actions and devious twists. There is never any important theme, and the plot shows only how the major characters manage to release themselves from entanglements.

Although farce often deals with illicit sexual relationships and infidelity, its outlook is amoral. Much of the fun is in the visual gags and absurdities of speech. The plot relies on misunderstandings, and many of the comic devices are used, including repetition, incongruity and derision.

One of the most successful writers of farce was Georges Feydeau, who wrote during the latter part of the nineteenth century and the beginning of the twentieth. One of his best-known plays is *A Flea in Her Ear,* which contrasts the respectability of the characters and the hypocrisy of their attitudes and actions.

There often are physical violence, misunderstandings, mistaken identity and deception. The characters are victims of their vices and appear ridiculous when caught, which they invariably are when they attempt to come together for illicit reasons, only to end up with the wrong person.

Tragicomedy

A genre which mingles elements of the comic and serious is tragicomedy. The term is paradoxical in that a protagonist who is truly tragic cannot appear comic, nor can a comic protagonist possess the scope of a tragic hero. Often a situation appears comic, but later the audience realizes it's serious. Tragicomedy generally tries to show how life intermingles the comic and the tragic. A good example is Harold Pinter's *The Birthday Party*, where bullies terrorize the central character Stanley. In Pinter's plays, characters' motivations are missing so that the audience often is unsure how to view their actions.

There are various other kinds of plays that do not seem to fit any particular genre. Some, such as *A Raisin in the Sun*, possess more scope than melodrama, yet do not end in the protagonist's defeat.

ACTIVITIES

1. What types of plays are you most interested in writing? What sort of audience would this most likely appeal to? What makes you think so?

2. What subjects are you particularly interested in that you could make interesting for an audience at a theatre?

3. Why do you want to write? Plays in particular? Would you rather write plays than novels or nonfiction? Why?

4. What is your main reason for attending plays? What do you hope to get out of seeing them? Any other reasons?

5. Investigate theatres in your area or city to see how many will consider accepting original scripts. If they do accept them, what are their conditions, their criteria, what they look for?

6. What genre of plays do you like most? Why?

143

CHAPTER 9

Characterization

The most memorable element of nearly all plays is the characters. If you ask people to tell you about a play they saw, they usually will say something like: "Well, it's about this guy who ..."

The characters are vehicles for the action, the theme, the progression of the plot. They usually determine the environment and the situations.

As you saw with the character interview, ideas for a play often can come from the development of a particular character.

KNOWING YOUR CHARACTERS

Generally, the more planning you do before starting the script, the easier it is, particularly if you are a beginning playwright. It helps to know more about your characters than will ever be revealed in the play. Think of characterization as a building with many sub-levels. A large part is buried below the surface, but there is a depth from which to draw. Because of a character's background and experiences, he or she will react believably, but differently from another character in any situation. To have your characters appear as three-dimensional human beings, you should know them as well as you can.

Often then when you put them in a scene, they seem to take the action into their own hands, which may give you some surprises. Yet you should find that what they did and said was logical.

Most successful plays focus on one character, for instance *Hamlet* and *Peer Gynt*, the latter a fantasy by Ibsen.

CHARACTER ANALYSIS

The things you need to know about your characters can be divided into five categories: 1) physical characteristics, 2) background, 3) attitudes and beliefs, 4) patterns of behavior and 5) dominant traits.

1. One of the first things is to figure out their physical attributes, such as height, weight, eye color and distinguishing features. Then try to determine what makes them individuals,

different from others of the same general type. What are their tastes in clothes? The character Rita in one of my plays, for instance, is "short and bouncy, with a false gaiety, assumed to convince herself she could have fun." She has brown, curly hair, cut short, and she wears tight-fitting dresses or sweaters and short skirts to make herself appear younger than she was. In the script I say: "She could have been pretty except that her features were too sharp, too pasted on with an overuse of makeup."

It is obvious that part of the physical appearance over which a character has some control will follow a certain pattern because of the character's feelings and attitudes about life. A director may see a character as physically different, and few actors will exactly fit your conception. But to create characters who are three-dimensional, it helps to visualize them.

2. Where did your characters grow up? Were their families rich or poor? How did this affect their outlook on life? How much schooling did they have? What are their interests and hobbies? What kind of work do they do? Are they happy with their jobs or would they rather be doing something else? If so, why?

What kinds of speech patterns do they have? Is their speech affected more by the location where they grew up, by their schooling or by their present environment? How does their speech reflect their personalities? What about vocal quality? What makes them sound the way they do? How are other people likely to view them? Are they likeable? Why, or why not? What were the biggest influences in their lives? What in their backgrounds has caused the biggest changes in their outlook? Are they basically optimistic or pessimistic, introverted or extroverted?

3. What are your characters' attitudes and beliefs about life in general? Why do they think this way? Was their early background strict, or did they have a lot of freedom? What influence did this have on them? Did the parents care about them? What was their parents' relationship with each other? How did parental attitudes, habits, living conditions and environment affect them? Do they like other people?

4. How do they act? Are they moody or generally happy? How are they likely to act in any given situation? Do they lead fairly structured lives or not? Why? Are they predictable?

146

5. Are they moral persons? What do they hope to accomplish in life? What are their main goals? What are their drives? How do they define success? Are they envious of others? Are they bitter toward life?

You need to take time with questions like these, really thinking about them. Analyze all of the major characters using questions like these and any others you think are important.

Remember that although characters generally believe one way, or react one way, in different situations, they may be just the opposite. Carl in my play *NHI: No Human Involved* hates homeless people. He loves his family. He contributes to causes to help poor people in other countries but will not help the needy people he sees everyday on the street. Later on, we discover that when Carl was a youngster, a man broke into his house and killed his mother because she wouldn't give the man money for drugs.

A story play deals with something that touches directly on the central character's past, that brings about reactions that might be different from people from a different type of background and different experiences. Willy Loman's past, including his brother's apparent success and Willy's own failures with instilling proper values in his sons, and his spending money on an illicit affair, all point up the fact that he is a failure, a belief further exacerbated by his doing worse and worse as a salesman. All of these things contribute to his obsession with being successful. He is driven by the past to achieve success which he defines in terms of money. Therefore, the only solution he sees is to kill himself so that his family will have the money from his life insurance.

His wife Linda cannot understand because their bills are paid, and they wouldn't have needed much to live on. She even says that he had the wrong dreams.

Willy's reaction is different from what anyone else's would be in similar circumstances. I cannot imagine, for instance, Grandpa in Kaufman and Hart's *You Can't Take It With You* committing suicide because he felt he had failed financially.

Nor can I imagine Willy Lomans ruthlessly trampling down anyone in his path to achieve success in the way that Regina does in Lillian Hellman's *The Little Foxes*. His experiences and personality are entirely different from hers. She, in turn, would never consider killing herself; she has too strong a personality. Nor can

147

I imagine Jack and Algernon in Oscar Wilde's *The Importance of Being Earnest* giving much attention to Willy's death, other than perhaps to refer to him as "that poor chap," or acknowledging the ruthlessness of a woman like Regina.

All this illustrates that each character you or anyone else create would react differently to any situation. Thus what may seem a logical choice for most people, isn't necessarily a logical choice for your character.

You've learned about various ways of creating and developing characters. It doesn't matter which method or combination of methods you use; all that matters is what works best for you.

Yet once you have the characters pretty well in mind, you might try writing monologs in which you ask them to tell you about something important to them. This could be an event that has had a lasting effect, a relationship or even what they want out of life. Here are a couple of monologs I developed this way. In the first instance, the monolog became a part of a longer work called *Tongues of Men and Angels*.

SETTING: A house in Southern California.

TIME: The present.

AT RISE: Martin, any age beyond 22 or 23, is talking to his best friend.

> **MARTIN:** You wonder why I never mentioned my folks. Okay, Frank, I'll tell you. They never wanted me. I was an unwelcome intruder, stealing pieces of their lives. I remember one time when I was a little kid, my mother accused me of trying to kill her by being born and of ruining her career as a musician. "Every time I tried to practice, you cried," she said. "You were a selfish little boy." And another time when I was no more than three or four, she packed her suitcase and said she was leaving and not coming back. I was such a horrible child, she said, that I didn't deserve a mother. She left, and I was all alone with no one to care how hard I cried. *(Exhales sharply.)*
>
> I wasn't allowed to call them Mom and Dad. They were Helen and Dan to me and everyone else.

You know, he was just as bad as she was, maybe even worse. When I was seventeen, just before Christmas in 1954, my senior year in high school, my grandparents came for a visit. Grandpa and I were sitting at the kitchen table talking about some evangelist or other, Billy Graham, I think. Anyhow, I said he was rich and should use all that money to help the poor. Grandpa disagreed, and I asked him to explain what he meant.

Dan was sitting in a chair up against the wall off to one side repairing a toaster or something. He told me to stop arguing, and I said we weren't; we were just talking. I turned back and started to say something else to Grandpa.

Dan jumped up and grabbed my arm and dragged me into the dining room. A powerful man, a good three inches shorter than I was, still he outweighed me. I tried to struggle free, but he slammed me into a corner, grabbed me around the neck and began to squeeze. At the same time he pounded my head — crack! crack! crack! — against the wall. Stop, I thought, oh, God, please stop! He'd hurt me before, but never like this. *(Swallows.)* My vision began to go like a gate being shut across my eyes, starting at the periphery and swinging in toward the center. I grabbed Dan's wrists and tried to pry his hands from around my neck. He only squeezed harder.

Helen was upstairs making up a bed for Grandma and Grandpa and must have heard the commotion. She came tearing down and into the dining room. "Dan!" she screamed running toward him and grabbing his arm. "Stop, for God's sake, stop! You're going to kill him." He released me then and stepped back.

I staggered forward and caught my balance. It felt like my throat was crushed, and there was this ring of white hot fire around my neck. I raced to the kitchen, grabbed my coat from a hook by the

149

door, shrugged into it, and stumbled outside and down the steps of the porch. The night was clear and cold; I was supposed to go caroling in Clivesville. I zipped up my jacket, ran down Second and turned up the hill. By the time I got to Sixth, I had the worst headache of my life, so bad it was making me ill. I slowed to a walk. *(Pause)*

I knew my father was frustrated; I knew money was scarce. Most of the kids who took music lessons had quit because their parents couldn't afford to pay him. But that wasn't my fault, damn it. My dad didn't need to take it out on me.

Anyhow, as I was thinking these things, I stopped for a moment, aware of the utter silence. No sound at all, not even the barking of a dog. I started trudging on again, the blades of grass at the side of the road breaking under my feet like thin glass. I knew I couldn't go caroling now, but I kept on walking toward Clivesville. My jacket had a fur collar; an aviator's jacket, maroon in color, and that soft fur rubbed my neck so bad I could hardly stand it. I unzipped the jacket and took it off. So what if I got sick? The wind whipped through the neck of my shirt like icy water rolling down my back.

What was I going to do when I got to Clivesville? I thought. What did it matter? Nobody cared; I wasn't sure I cared myself. I thought: my father always treats me like worthless — my mother too. So maybe I am worthless. And I thought maybe I'd freeze to death and that would be that. Or I'd get hit by a car. Maybe I'd try to help things along. I fluffed my jacket into a pillow and laid it on the white center line of that macadam road, old Route 30, the Lincoln Highway. So I lay down, my head in the middle of the jacket, and drew my legs up to my chest and closed my eyes. I figured if I were lucky, it would all end quickly. But nothing happened. After awhile I opened my eyes. My breath hung in the air like a trail of ghostly balloons. Occasionally, a leaf blew by, or I heard a far-off car horn. I began to shake. The running and the walking had made me sweat, and the sweat was beginning to freeze. Time passed as in a dream, and I don't know how long I lay there. *(Laughs harshly.)*

For the first time, ever or since, I'll bet, that damned road stayed empty, and I got tired of waiting to die. I sat up and looked off in the distance at the trees making stark silhouettes against the light of the moon and the stars twinkling hundreds of light years away, some maybe even dead but their light still streaming down. So anyhow I stood up, put on my jacket and kept on walking. *(Pause)*

So what do you think, Frank? Would I have let a car run over me if one had come along? I didn't know then, and I don't know now. But I seriously doubt that I would have. I never really wanted to die ... did I? Sometimes I had trouble knowing what was real and what was only my imagination.

Pretty soon I got to Clivesville and went to see Thelma and Dick Polsky. They used to live next door. Dick was at the VFW, and Thelma wouldn't believe me when I told her what had happened. So I gulped this glass of water she handed me and stumbled outside.

I'd walked eleven miles already, and it was late. I was just a kid. Seventeen years old. So I hiked back home. I told myself that if I kept up a steady pace, it wouldn't take more than a couple of hours. But that seemed like an eternity. You see, the fatigue made me colder than ever. I had no reserves to fight it. So I just kept plodding along, left foot, right foot, left foot, right foot, each step jarring my body. But I made it, Frank. The whole damn way.

I stopped then and leaned against the board fence, and I was filled with hate. I opened the gate and staggered up onto the front porch. The door wouldn't be locked; it never was, and I saw that

151

someone had left the lamp on low. It was Grandma. She sat there, her face in near darkness. "Oh, Martin," she said. "I'm sorry." You know, there was nothing else that she could say. Really now, was there?

The second monolog is not an end in itself. Instead, it helped only to develop a scene for a play.

SEAN: Mom had a surprise party for me last year on my birthday. I was seventeen. She sent me to Rick's house to ask if he'd like to go out to dinner and then to a movie to help celebrate. When I was gone, the other kids came to the house. All my friends from school.

Rick and I walked into the living room, and everyone yelled, "Surprise." Then we went to the grove out back to build a fire for a wiener roast, and I started to open my presents. We heard a loud crash and ran to the highway. There was a car in the field up the hill. We ran to see if we could help. The car had crashed through a barbed-wire fence and lay on its roof. A man screamed, "My legs! Oh, my God, my legs!" He was on the driver's side, and someone sat beside him. The roof was crumpled, and we couldn't tell anything about the other person, just that his chest was covered with blood.

Someone said that maybe we should try to get the two men out because the car might explode. Rick said maybe we should wait for an ambulance. Then the driver started to cry. "Please, fellows," he said. "Oh, God, please." So Bob said we should place ourselves around the car, and he called out, "One, two, three, lift."

I was on the passenger side, and Jesus God, this guy was lying there with his head against the roof. And his head was cut off, hanging from a little bit of skin in back. I started to puke and choke, but somehow I held onto the car. A couple of my friends pulled the other man out. His legs were smashed and twisted all weird-like. Someone ran to call an ambulance, and we all went back home, except for Bob who said he'd wait till the ambulance came.

We were all sitting around in the living room, not talking or anything. And one of the girls — Sally, I think it was — said that since the fire was going good out back, we might as well have our wiener roast. So we all went out there and tried not to think about the guys up in the field.

We sat around the fire, and it was almost dark, and we tried to pretend that nothing had happened. It's almost a year now, and I can still see this guy's head just hanging there, and the blood — And I'll always remember my seventeenth birthday.

Once you establish your characters, examine their relationships. You need to determine how each makes the others feel during each scene and how they react together. If characters do not affect each other in any way whatsoever, one or more of them should not be there.

All characters, no matter how minor, are attempting to accomplish something. In effect, each has an obstacle, a phone he or she sets out to fix, a package that needs to be delivered. These, of course, are very minor. Yet they are included to reach a certain goal. If they do not have a purpose in any given scene, they do not belong in that scene.

Neither should a character simply mark time on stage. He or she has to have a purpose other than simply waiting for another character to finish a monolog or physical action. It's not important to explore background and motivation for minor characters; it only detracts from the plot or confuses the audience, who expect to see them play a more important part in the outcome.

If characters in a play do not either help the protagonist or somehow block his or her way, at least temporarily, there's no point in their being included.

For instance, even the soldiers, who are totally non-entities in *Marching in Time*, have the goal of capturing and guarding the Man, the Woman, and the Driver.

Any time you bring characters on stage, they should be

striving to fulfill some intention or reach some goal, which, most often is in conflict with that of the protagonist or sometimes with the other central characters. The soldiers collectively in *Marching in Time* are really only one character because they behave almost in unison and have no distinguishing characteristics. They do not need to be developed because they are only devices. Therefore, you wouldn't want to give any of them dialog beyond the very basic.

This brings up an important point. Characters must react and speak according to their purpose and their relationships with each other.

The soldiers probably do not know the other characters, and even if they did, they would not attempt to carry on a conversation with them.

On the other hand, Joe and Nadine in *NHI: No Human Involved* do know each other, and this is reflected in their conversation. For instance, Joe would have no reason to explain to her that he is an ex-policeman, ex-street person who now has his own detective agency. On the other hand, he might need to explain this to someone else he's trying to get to help him solve the murders, someone he has never met or whom he knows slightly. This means that when two characters know each other well, as do Joe and Nadine, they cannot logically fill each other in on background details as a way of providing exposition for an audience. It would be silly, for instance, to have a scene like this in a play:

John: Well, here we are, the first day of our vacation, and we forgot to ask the Thompsons to water our plants while we're gone.
Marsha: Yes, and, like we discussed, we should have asked them to collect any papers left on our porch.
John: Oh, well, since this is the first vacation we've taken in the last eight years, we should just try to forget such things and enjoy our two weeks together.
Marsha: Yes, as you know, I think it's terrible that the office never let you have time off until now.
John: We've discussed that, Marsha. At first, we didn't have enough employees to keep things going, and then ...

154

On the other hand, you could bring out some of the same information unobtrusively, while giving the scene more conflict. This in turn makes it more interesting.

MARSHA: For heaven's sake, John, how could you forget to give the Thompsons the key?

JOHN: I had a lot on my mind, okay?

MARSHA: *(Sarcastically)* Important stuff, huh?

JOHN: Look, Marsha, I'm taking the damned vacation, okay? It's against my better judgment. But I said I would, so I will. Besides, I couldn't stand your bitching anymore.

MARSHA: My bitching! Who complains about how hard he has to work all the time? I'd think you'd want a vacation. All I asked was one little thing, give the Thompsons the key while I finished packing.

JOHN: They're your plants, babe! I don't give a damn if they're watered or not —

MARSHA: Thirteen more days of this! How can I stand it! *(Glaring at him)* Why should I even try!

JOHN: You don't have to try. I don't know if Roy can handle things at the office. I'd just as soon go home.

MARSHA: What is it with you? Can't you think of anything but your precious —

JOHN: Well, for eight years, babe, it's given us the money to live on. And live pretty well I might add.

MARSHA: Will you stop calling me babe! *(Sighs.)* Ah, Johnny, I know how much the business means to you. I just thought it was time to get away. I hate to see you work so hard. I know you had to at first, when you and Roy were starting up. But don't you realize I love you? You're more important to me ... than the business, the plants —

JOHN: *(Throwing back his head and laughing)* More important than the plants! Now that's good to know.

Each of your major characters, like each person you know, should be unique — complete human beings whose actions can be understood, although not necessarily condoned.

If you are having trouble in understanding one of them or understanding his or her motives, you can do another character interview, this time stressing a particular facet of the personality.

WRITER: Which is more important to you, John, your wife or your business? I never did know for sure.
CHARACTER: That's a tough one. I know what you'd like me to say. I know what I should say.
WRITER: Your wife?
CHARACTER: Yeah, but I'm not really sure. Doesn't make me very likeable, does it?
WRITER: I still like you. You're a good guy; you pretty much try to do what's right.
CHARACTER: I suppose so.
WRITER: But you don't sound too sure.
CHARACTER: Naw.
WRITER: Is that depression, I hear?
CHARACTER: My mom and dad always taught me that family came first. It did for them.
WRITER: And you're feeling guilty about it?
CHARACTER: I'm feeling guilty.
WRITER: So what are you going to do?
CHARACTER: Keep on going, I guess. Keep feeling this way till something happens.
WRITER: Some sort of conflict, you mean?
CHARACTER: Isn't that what this is all about? My torn allegiance.
WRITER: Maybe it is, John. I hadn't thought of that. I thought it was more about the pressures of business, the little guy starting up.
CHARACTER: There's that too. But that's just one of the symptoms, one of the complications.
WRITER: So what are we going to do?
CHARACTER: Put Marsha and me together to face some crisis?
WRITER: Anything in mind?
CHARACTER: Roy's cheating me big-time. Marsha's upset 'cause I spend so little time with her. Maybe she gets drunk, has an accident.
WRITER: Maybe, but isn't that sort of trite?
CHARACTER: Handled the right way, maybe not. You're the playwright. The issue has to be brought to a head — the business versus Marsha. I have to be tested. Then we'll see what happens.

156

Creating characters is a subjective process. The things you write are your perceptions of the world. They show how you feel and what you believe. So even though your characters are unique and complex, they still will be the product of the way you think and believe.

At the same time they are unique, characters should have universal qualities, traits and feelings with which we all can identify.

Of course, it would be nearly impossible to find a character who is completely alien. Each of us has the basis or potential for developing nearly every personality trait. Other people may have talents or abilities we don't. Still, we relate to them.

If somehow we could go back in time and arrange a different set of circumstances for our early lives, we probably would be a lot different than we are now, and maybe more like some others. There are bits of everyone's character traits in us, and bits of ours in everyone else. We aren't all killers, but in certain circumstances maybe we could be, to protect something important to us.

You also need to consider that murderers have positive traits with which others can sympathize. You need to find these traits in your characters and then portray them. Otherwise, they'll come across as unbelievable, either totally good or totally bad. And they won't be interesting.

All characters have to be stereotyped or typified to a certain extent for the audience to be able to identify with them. This usually means only that the character has to possess universal qualities. If the audience sees someone who appears to be of a type with whom they can identify, they will have no trouble in assuming certain things about the person. You don't need to express them openly. For example, the audience could safely assume that a typical mother and father would be concerned about their children. If they are not typical, you need to be sure the audience knows this.

On the other hand, if the major characters don't have distinctive traits of their own, things that set them apart from others, they won't be believable. In creating a character, you need

157

to have a balance between typification and individuality.

DETERMINING IMPORTANT TRAITS

You need to decide what character traits you want to emphasize. Although you may know your central characters fully, the audience doesn't or can't. There isn't time. So even though your major characters should come across as complex, they have to be simpler than people in real life so the audience can easily grasp what they are like.

In certain ways novelists have an advantage over playwrights. They can write long paragraphs describing people's motives and actions. The expository material in a play can be brought about only through appearance or dialog. Novelists can write as many pages of text as they wish. As a playwright you have about two hours' playing time, so obviously you need to be selective. If you try to show too much about a character, the result will be confusing or vague. Decide what traits are most important for your characters to have in striving toward whatever goal you've established for them. Then make sure those traits are apparent to an audience.

CHOOSING THE NUMBER OF CHARACTERS

You should include only those characters necessary to advance the plot. It's hard enough to present a few traits of one character without introducing a lot of unnecessary persons who have wants and needs of their own. Each extra character takes away from the time that can be spent with the major character.

Yet, it's difficult to write a two-character play because you need other characters for these to play off. You need other characters as sounding boards.

Another general rule is that the characters in tragedies usually are developed more fully than those in comedies. We might feel hesitant about laughing at someone whom we know well and with whom we identify.

CHOOSING SCENES FOR THE CENTRAL CHARACTERS

To provide interest, to build suspense and to hold attention, all the scenes in a play should be important. Anything not essential to the plot only detracts. This means you should begin as close to the climax as possible.

There are several ways of revealing a character in a scene. One is through dialog among other characters. But we don't learn much about others just by hearing about them. People's views of others are colored by their own personalities, so we can't rely on what we're told. We have to meet people to find out what they're like. We must see people doing something or hear them talk before we can tell much about them.

The best way to learn to know a character is to see the person acting and reacting. The best way of revealing or portraying characters is to present them in conflict. We learn about them by the way they meet crises. We discover the most, for instance, about Walter Younger in *A Raisin in the Sun* by seeing him in conflict with the neighborhood representative who wants to pay him for not moving into a white community.

We can tell a lot about the characters in a play by what they do when their goals or drives are opposed. And there may be some surprises.

When the opposition becomes the strongest, the most important qualities of the character will be revealed. We see how far a character will go to achieve an aim.

This is the sort of situation in which basic personality is best revealed. One of the main objectives in revealing character in this way is to hold the attention of the audience, and the best way to hold that attention is to make the spectator want to know how the character will respond. We want to see what lengths Oedipus will go to in trying to end the plague in Thebes and why he persists even after he realizes the search for the murderer of Laius will end in his own destruction.

REVEALING CHARACTER

We learn more about each important character the more we see him or her, just as we learn more about a person in real life the more often we meet. If an audience knows everything at first, including how a character is likely to react in a crisis, there won't be much to sustain their interest.

So you need to reveal character bit by bit. In each new scene, a part of a character's personality that wasn't previously

159

apparent is now revealed. Characters in plays do not undergo great personality changes (unless they are brainwashed!). They may change their minds, the way they act or even their goals. But such changes are brought about by something already a part of their makeup. It's often been said that adversity best shows a person's true mettle. When faced with trouble, the strong often become weak and the weak become strong. A character in a play is no different.

The point is that you should push your central characters to their limits to see how they react. Then show how this affects them — if they learn anything important, if they will modify their behavior for the better.

Do be careful not to make your characters too predictable. Give them some secrets, some interesting facets, not at first apparent.

Often a character can be identified or made real in the audience's mind through physical actions. Even when engaged in conversation or conflict, a man who continuously polishes and arranges his collection of antique bottles will come across differently than a man who constantly cleans and oils his antique gun collection. Yet nothing need be mentioned in the dialog about either action.

A repeated action — constantly straightening magazines and other objects around a room — can tell us a lot about a person, or about the circumstances of the scene.

Another point to keep in mind in writing scenes for your characters is that just as we play roles in real life, characters play different roles with different people and in different situations. A man will play a different role with his co-workers than with his young children. He will "become" another person in his bowling league.

DETERMINING THE PLAY'S OUTCOME

The climax of a good play has to be logical in light of what has happened and in light of the characters' psychological makeup. We know that the two main characters in Neil Simon's *Barefoot in the Park* will "live happily ever after" despite obvious differences in outlook and background. We know this because of their love for each other, which is the most important emotion felt by either. Since the play is a comedy, the audiences knows

160

things will work out. The suspense is concerned with *how* this will happen.

In your own plays, try to include situations that will best reveal the dominant traits of your characters. For instance, if a man has an overwhelming drive to succeed at his job, he can be placed in a situation where this drive can be tested. He is one of three people being considered for a promotion. How does this affect him? Put him in situations with the other two people being considered and find out.

How does John react to Marsha's accusations that he's spending too much time at the office to the detriment of his family? How does he react differently when the issue of overtime comes up again during a conversation with his partner Roy?

Seeds for any important action have to be planted ahead of time. The characters not only speak to themselves but also foresee situations in which they may later be placed.

Take care in choosing characters' names. They should be appropriate. For example, "Jim" may suggest an honest, straightforward person, while "Algernon" seems to imply an affected, artsy type. Consider a name's connotations. The more common the name, the less connotations it will have.

ACTIVITIES

1. Determine the type of character that would likely become involved in one of the following situations and then decide what about personality or background would cause the character to react in a particular way to it. Remember that there are many type of characters who likely would be involved in these situations, but there are others who would simply walk away from them.

A. A person facing financial ruin because of a bad investment. You might consider probable reasons for the investment, and what action the person might take to rectify the situation.

B. A person torn between protecting personal privacy and exposing a major scandal. Consider how and why the person knows about the scandal, and the likely results of either decision.

C. A person given the opportunity to try something he or

she has wanted to do since childhood. But the person has to give up a secure position. Consider that whatever choice is made, there's no going back.

Write a short character sketch of a person likely to be involved in one of the foregoing situations and what course of action he or she would logically take to get out of it. Remember that the character has to consider everything that's at stake. How will it affect him or her personally? How will it affect friends or family? What will be the long-term consequences?

At the same time, write a sketch of a character — including background and personality traits — who simply would not be affected or would not even become involved in such a situation. Be specific in determining the traits of both characters and in proving that they would have absolutely opposite reactions to the situation.

2. Take a character you've already developed or start with a new one, and do a detailed analysis of the character's goals, needs, drives and motives, as well as background, current situation, personality traits and physical appearance.

3. Develop and analyze in the same way two or three secondary characters who might react with the central character you have developed.

4. Analyze the relationship among your characters and develop a situation in which you could place a combination of two or more of these characters.

5. Write a scene based on the situation you have developed.

6. Write another scene that will effectively reveal an important trait of the central character.

7. Write a third scene that would be a logical outcome of one of the other two scenes you have written.

CHAPTER 10

Dialog

Dialog has three main functions: to reveal character, to create atmosphere and to advance the plot. To accomplish these purposes:

1. It has to have clarity;

2. It has to be appropriate to the character, the situation, and the setting;

3. It has to be natural.

Clarity means that no matter how uneducated the character, or no matter how strong an accent or dialect, the audience should not have to strain to understand what the characters are saying. At the same time, it has to be easy for the actors to say.

The dialog has to be appropriate to the character's background, and you need to keep in mind that characters will speak differently to different people, e.g., when they are playing different roles such as parent or employee, and when they are feeling different emotions. A person also would speak differently, for instance, at a memorial service than at a birthday party. In other words, dialog has to show feeling.

The dialog has to sound natural. That is, it has to fit the character. In everyday life, for instance, some people are more hesitant than others. Some are shy, others outgoing. Some are bombastic; others have a quiet forcefulness. Take all these things into consideration for each of your characters in each scene of a play.

Consider that since most plays present the actors as real people in real situations, the dialog has to sound like everyday speech.

What does this mean? Nobody speaks the same way as anyone else. People in one part of the country have slightly different vocal patterns and inflections than those in other parts. Expressions heard in one place may be unusual in another. Even people who grew up in the same area and have similar backgrounds speak differently due to different interests or personalities. So how can you know what is natural and appropriate? First, the dialog should be natural to the character. How would the character speak? Why? A lot of this is determined by the character analysis. If the character is stuffy, he or she will probably speak in a stilted way, whereas an informal person wouldn't do this, even though the two of them have similar backgrounds. Dialog should help show the audience the type of person the character is.

Environment helps determines the way a character speaks. Children of foreign-born parents, particularly if they live among others of the same nationality, imitate the speech they hear and so have an accent. It's common for a Northerner to live in the South for a few months and acquire the beginnings of a southern accent.

The extent of a person's schooling contributes to speech patterns and habits. Someone with little schooling may not use good grammar and may not have the vocabulary to express thoughts as coherently as a person with more formal education. On the other hand, the person with little formal training may compensate by speaking more carefully or precisely.

LEARNING TO HEAR SPEECH PATTERNS

One of the best ways of learning to write believable dialog is learning to hear it. Try to figure out why one person talks differently from another. Part of the first impression you gain from people is from their speech. Analyze what makes you conclude certain things about them, and then try to figure out if the conclusions are justifiable.

Try recording conversations among college students having a bull session, between two workers coming home on a bus, or between two old people grocery shopping. Then take the conversations and try to extend them, using the same vocal patterns and style that you've recorded. The two shoppers may be complaining about high prices. Try to figure out why. Are they on fixed incomes? Are they complaining because they cannot afford some of the luxuries they would like, or is it only that such complaints are an expected "ritual" to help pass each day? Maybe they feel that such a subject is safe ground. They can speak about something that *seems* important in order to avoid something that *is*. As you know, people often mean to imply other things than what they actually say. For example, it probably would be embarrassing for both you and your friend if you went up to the person one day and announced, "I really like you a lot. I think you're the best friend I've ever had, and I treasure our times together." But you tell the person the same thing in more subtle ways.

When you listen to others speak and then extend the conversation, try to imagine the facial expressions and body movements that go along with the words. Body language can tell a lot about a person's character and the way he or she is feeling. Often it directly contradicts the words.

DIFFERENCES BETWEEN EVERYDAY SPEECH AND DIALOG

Most conversations tend to ramble and change directions quickly. They often are merely social and thus inconsequential in content. People want to have contact with one another, but they don't want to run the risk of being rejected by stating innermost feelings. So they compromise and talk to each other about trivial things.

On the stage, dialog has to have a purpose. Even when the main point of a particular play is lack of communication, the dialog has to be selective. *The Bald Soprano* takes the everyday lack of awareness and makes it appear more absurd than it is. People usually are able to recognize their husbands or wives, and they don't become shocked over someone's tying a shoelace, as the couples do in Ionesco's play.

Dialog makes a point. It's not as repetitive as normal conversations where words, phrases and ideas may be repeated several times. Unless the situation demands it, or it is for emphasis or character portrayal, dialog is much less redundant than everyday speech. This is true in order to establish a character quickly and advance the plot.

RULES OF WRITING DIALOG

Forced cleverness and flowery language tend to grate on the nerves of the audience. On the other hand, forget any rules of dialog in establishing or portraying character. When you write a play, do include the language that suits the character, but don't overdo it, or the dialog starts to call attention to itself.

A theatre audience doesn't have time to reflect upon each speech. This means the dialog has to be clear and understandable on first hearing, even though the characters use improper grammar or speak with an accent. In a practical sense, this means using simple sentences, rather than those that are long and convoluted.

Dialog needs to have a natural rhythm and flow, which help establish mood and atmosphere. It should fit the emotional content of the scenes and the emotions of the characters. As you saw in Chapter 5, the more passive the emotion, the longer and smoother the sentences and speeches. The higher the emotional pitch, the more staccato and abrupt the dialog. This corresponds to real life situations.

Long speeches, though at times necessary, do slow down the action.

How many different things, for instance, can you infer about each of the situations and characters from the following dialog?

1. Well, I don't really know if that's the appropriate thing to do. I mean, would she appreciate having a surprise party? I know I wouldn't. It's ... But I guess we're speaking about her, aren't we? Not about me.

2. You know, I'm thirty-two years old. Yet I often think of a promise my father made and broke when I was a kid: to give me a ride in a plane for my birthday. I wanted to do it so badly, like I belonged in the sky flying like a huge bird, not tied to earth. Not tied to what things were like. But every birthday came and went, and there was never a ride.

3. Oh, we gonna shake hands? You don't think I'm gonna pollute you with some nasty disease or somethin' like that. You know how filthy street people are.

4. For heaven's sake, can't you be more careful! I don't know what gets into you. We don't have money to buy new cups.

5. Some of us weren't so lucky as you. You had your Fred. I had nobody.

PURPOSES OF DIALOG

Dialog gives information essential to each scene and to the play as a whole. It's the way that most expository material is delivered. (The other ways are through sets, lighting, costuming and possibly makeup.) But the exposition shouldn't intrude upon the progress of the play. The audience needs to receive information without being aware that they are receiving it. It should seem a natural part of the conversation. Consider, for instance, this scene from Oscar Wilde's *The Importance of Being Earnest.*

ALGERNON: How are you, my dear Earnest? What brings you up to town?

JACK: Oh, pleasure, pleasure! What else should bring one anywhere? Eating as usual, I see, Algy!

ALGERNON: *(Stiffly)* I believe it is customary in good society to take some slight refreshment at five o'clock. Where have you been since last Thursday?

JACK: *(Sitting down on the sofa)* In the country.

ALGERNON: What on earth do you do there?

JACK: *(Pulling off his gloves)* When one is in town one amuses oneself. When one is in the country one amuses other people. It is excessively boring.

ALGERNON: And who are the people you amuse?

JACK: *(Airily)* Oh, neighbours, neighbours.

ALGERNON: Got nice neighbours in your part of Shropshire?

JACK: Perfectly horrid! Never speak to them.

ALGERNON: How immensely you must amuse them! *(Goes over and takes a sandwich.)* By the way, Shropshire is your county, is it not?

JACK: Eh? Shropshire? Yes, of course. Hallo! Why all these cups? Why cucumber sandwiches? Why such reckless extravagance in one so young? Who is coming to tea?

ALGERNON: Oh! merely Aunt Augusta and Gwendolen.

JACK: How perfectly delightful!

ALGERNON: Yes, that is all very well; but I am afraid Aunt Augusta won't quite approve of your being here.

JACK: May I ask why?

ALGERNON: My dear fellow, the way you flirt with Gwendolen is perfectly disgraceful. It is almost as bad as the way Gwendolen flirts with you.

JACK: I am in love with Gwendolen. I have come up to town expressly to propose to her.

ALGERNON: I thought you had come up for pleasure? . . . I call that business.

JACK: How utterly unromantic you are!

ALGERNON: I really don't see anything romantic in proposing. It is very romantic to be in love. But there is nothing romantic about a definite proposal. Why, one may be accepted. One usually is, I believe. Then the excitement is all over. The very essence of romance is uncertainty. If ever I get married, I'll certainly try to forget the fact.

Wilde gives the audience a lot of information in a very entertaining way. First, we can surmise that Jack and Algernon are friends — fairly close since Jack has apparently dropped in unexpectedly. We can tell a lot about the social standing of the two. We know that Algernon is soon going to serve tea to Gwendolen and his aunt. We learn that Jack probably loves Gwendolen and the feelings are reciprocated. We learn something about the men's views, and seeds are planted for future events and conflicts, e.g., a scene between Aunt Augusta and Jack.

Wilde presents the scene through a series of little conflicts. Rather than having Jack merely enter and talk about where he's been, Wilde brings out all the information in a series of small disagreements which, though not serious, do maintain our interest. For example, Algernon is somewhat accusatory in asking where Jack has been. Then through his line, "What on earth do you do there?" we can infer that he doesn't particularly like the country. The lines are humorous also because they are unexpected. All of this reveals not only setting and circumstances, but gives us information about the kind of people Jack and Algernon are.

Dialog advances the theme of the play. Largely through what is said, an audience is able to tell what direction the play is taking. We can easily see by reading the excerpt from *The Importance of Being Earnest* that the play will be a drawing room comedy, and that we are not to take the characters and situation seriously. We also can see that the theme probably will have something to do with romance or love.

What sorts of things can you tell about the characters and the situation in the following scene from William Gillette's nineteenth century play *Secret Service*? What type of person is Wilfred? Mrs. Varney?

WILFRED: *(right center)* It hasn't stopped altogether — don't you hear?
MRS. VARNEY: *(center)* Yes, but compared to what it was yesterday — you know it shook the house. Howard suffered

dreadfully! *(WILFRED suddenly faces her.)*
WILFRED: So did I, Mother! *(Slight pause) (Low boom of cannon)*
MRS. VARNEY: YOU!
WILFRED: When I hear those guns and know the fighting's on, it makes me —
MRS. VARNEY: *(Goes toward table left center. Interrupting quickly)* Yes, yes — we all suffered — we all suffered, dear! *(Sits right of table L.C.)*
WILFRED: Mother — you may not like it but you must listen — *(going toward her)* — you must let me tell you how —
MRS. VARNEY: Wilfred! *(He stops speaking. — She takes his hand in hers tenderly. — A brief pause)* I know.
WILFRED: *(Low pleading voice)* But it's true, Mother! I can't stay back here any longer! It's worse than being shot to pieces! I can't do it. *(MRS. VARNEY looks steadily into WILFRED's face but says nothing. Soon she turns away a little as if she felt tears coming into her eyes.)* Why don't you speak?
MRS. VARNEY: *(Turning to him. A faint attempt to smile)* I don't know what to say.
WILFRED: Say you won't mind if I go down there and help 'em.
MRS. VARNEY: It wouldn't be true!
WILFRED: I can't stay here!
MRS. VARNEY: You're so young!
WILFRED: No younger then Tom Kittridge — no younger than Ell Stuart — nor cousin Stephen — nor hundreds of the fellows fighting down there! — See Mother — they've called for all over eighteen — that was weeks ago! The seventeen call may be out any minute — the next one after that takes me! Do I want to stay back here till they order me out? I should think not! *(Walks about to C. Stops and speaks to MRS. VARNEY.)* If I was hit with a shell an' had to stay it would be different! But I can't stand this — I can't do it Mother!

BUILDING SUSPENSE AND INTENSITY

As you know, a play has to build. This means not telling everything at once. In everyday life, people don't usually give others a lot of information in a single exchange, unless someone is asking directions, for instance. So in this way, dialog in a play

169

is like conversation. Besides, you have a play's entire structure to develop plot, to heighten moments of tension, to build suspense and to reveal character.

Not only does parceling out the information a bit at a time create suspense, but it holds the audience's interest. An audience simply cannot absorb a lot of information in a short burst. They'll stop paying attention. Theatregoers don't want to work at understanding a play. They want the work done for them.

In conversation and in life there is a natural ebb and flow. The same should be true with the dialog and with the action of a play. Even when two people are in a lengthy, heated quarrel, the emotions don't remain at one pitch of intensity. No actor and no person in everyday life can maintain intense emotion for a long period of time. Carrying the dialog at too high an emotional pitch throughout a scene makes the play lose meaning. There's no way to build further. So the intensity has to be highlighted. Contrasts provide emphasis and give the scene more impact, the final attack more power.

It's just as bad to have a scene change emotions too quickly or too often. What is supposed to be serious will then seem funny. If your audience is confused about the kind of response expected, you have defeated your purpose.

CHARACTER RELATIONSHIPS

Keep in mind the sort of relationship the characters have with each other, particularly how well they know each other. For instance, you wouldn't have a conversation like the first one that follows between two men who've been friends, as well as business associates, for years.

Nor would you have the second conversation between two men who know each other slightly and in a business situation.

Conversation 1

BOB: Mr. Grimm, it's good to see you. I trust you had a pleasant trip.
PETE We were late taking off, but other than that the trip went well enough. *(Shaking hands)* It's good to see you too, Bennet. It's been awhile. I suppose the last time was when we worked together on the Raphael deal.

170

BOB: So how have you been?

PETE: Fine, and you? If I remember correctly, the last time we met you mentioned taking up skiing. You and your wife?

BOB: I'm flattered that you remember. Actually, we've found we really enjoy it. It's a great way to spend a weekend. And Betsy's parents are happy to keep the two kids for us.

PETE: As you may remember, my wife and I ski too.

Conversation 2

BOB: Hey, man, it's good to see you. How was the trip?

PETE: Fine. Bit of a delay due to the weather, that's all. Been a long time, huh?

BOB: Since the Raphael deal, can you believe it?

PETE: So how's the skiing going? You told me last time that you and Betsy —

BOB: You remember that, huh? We love it. It's always good to get away for awhile. No worries, no responsibilities. And the kids love staying with Betsy's folks.

PETE: Know what you mean. Nothin' in the world like it. Out on the slopes, the sense of freedom.

If two people know each other, their dialog has a lot of shortcuts because there's no need for explanations, often no need for formality. In fact, the two examples should be reversed. A character wouldn't presume such familiarity with someone he doesn't know.

What sorts of relationships do you think the characters have in the following two scenes? What can you tell about the characters themselves?

Scene 1

(The action takes place in BRAD's ceramic studio.)

BRAD: So what do you think?

FRANK: Sissy job, that's what I think.

BRAD: Yeah, Frank. The Japanese who've been doing this for centuries are sissies. The Greeks were sissies. All the —

FRANK: All right, you convinced me.

BRAD: You're just saying that because you care.

FRANK: God, you must have hundreds of dollars tied up in this.

BRAD: You could say that. You could also say thousands.

FRANK: Why?

171

BRAD: Why? Because I enjoy it. Because I'm good at it.

FRANK: How good?

BRAD: I'll show you. *(He hands FRANK a newspaper clipping.)* Take a look.

FRANK: *(Reading)* "Bradley Booth, one of Southern California's most promising ceramists, has developed truly innovative methods of ... *(He looks up.)* Why in the hell are you a waiter then?

BRAD: To support my habit.

FRANK: What?

BRAD: My addiction to clay.

FRANK: You mean you don't earn enough money —

BRAD: Someday, Frank. But I want to be sure I can make it first. It's hard being a full-time potter or ceramist. And I had all this equipment to buy.

FRANK: What is all this stuff?

BRAD: Kiln, extruder, grinder, pugger —

FRANK: What does that mean?

BRAD: Later, Frank.

FRANK: Maybe not.

BRAD: Oh, yeah?

FRANK: Sissy stuff.

BRAD: Let's try a little bit. *(He grabs two plastic bags of red clay and hands them to FRANK who can barely hold them.)*

FRANK: These bags are heavy.

BRAD: Naw. Just your regular sissy size.

SCENE 2

(SAM and MARTIN are sitting at the kitchen table.)

SAM: A penny for your thoughts.

MARTIN: I was thinking about what Ray told me before I joined the troop.

SAM: About what?

MARTIN: About you.

SAM: *(Laughing)* What about me?

MARTIN: How you used to be a policeman. *(Pause)* Uncle Stanley said that ... that I probably shouldn't mention it.

SAM: About my ... injury? My leg?

MARTIN: He said you might get upset.

SAM: It's part of my life. It's hard to talk about. But someone did try to kill me.

172

MARTIN: You were a policeman. A detective.

SAM: For almost four years. On the force for nine years.

MARTIN: Wow.

SAM: Not so long. *(Peering closely at MARTIN)* That looks like a nasty bump on your head.

MARTIN: *(Softly)* Yeah.

SAM: Fall down? *(Pause)* Was that it?

MARTIN: Something like that. *(SAM doesn't answer.)* My head hit the wall. *(Looking into SAM'S eyes)* It's okay.

SAM: So I hear you're a pretty good trumpet player, huh?

MARTIN: If you mean senior band, yeah, I am. Only one other eighth grader got chosen. My friend Bobbie Thomas. She plays clarinet.

SAM: Sounds like your music's important.

MARTIN: I want to be in the Marine Band. Someday. Or have a dance band, like Harry James. Except ...

SAM: Except what?

MARTIN: My dad thinks it's wrong. My mom too. Dancing and stuff.

SAM: I used to be a musician.

MARTIN: You did?

SAM: The organ. Started fooling around with it in the church we attended. The organist gave me lessons. When she quit, I took over.

MARTIN: Do you still play?

SAM: *(Shaking his head)* No.

MARTIN: Why?

SAM: Long story. *(MARTIN's face loses animation; he retreats inside himself. After a moment)* The accident, Martin. But every time I step into the church for a Scout meeting, it's like I'm drawn to it. Like a magnet's pulling me up the steps and into the sanctuary. Maybe I'll talk to the preacher.

PHYSICAL ACTIVITY

Pantomime or physical activity can be as effective as dialog, as evidenced by such plays as Mark Medoff's *Children of a Lesser God* or William Gibson's *The Miracle Worker*, both of which have deaf characters who do not or cannot speak.

If characters become frustrated or angry, let the audience see them venting their emotions rather than talking about them.

Physical action, as well as dialog, has to be appropriate. If the characters are in a state of mild anxiety or tension, they may straighten pictures or fuss with their hair. If they are experiencing strong anxiety, the actions are stronger. You shouldn't plan out every detail of movement (because that's up to the director and actors), but you should be able to visualize the characters in action. Just as you wouldn't force dialog upon the characters in order to control the direction of a scene, neither should you force physical action upon them. It should grow out of the characterization and fit the personality.

IDENTIFYING WITH YOUR CHARACTERS

It's hard to establish credibility or to present three-dimensional characters whose dialog and actions are believable if you cannot identify with or understand them. In *The Writing of One Novel: The Prize* Irving Wallace says that when he stops writing to eat dinner with his family, he often is somewhat shocked not to see his characters sitting around the table. He has identified so closely with them that they have become real people.

REVISING THE DIALOG

After you've written dialog for a scene, you need to revise it. Rarely does something turn out exactly right in the first draft. You need to cut, add or change. This is more of an intellectual exercise because you need to be aware of the technical aspects of structure, of developing sentences that make sense and of cutting out what is unnecessary.

You have to heighten the effectiveness of the scenes and possibly interject dialog for clarification. You have to be analytical while retaining the feeling of the scene.

Try to judge the dialog's overall effectiveness. Does it portray personality as well as it should? Does it sound as natural as possible? Does it suit the character and his or her feelings at the time? Try to read the play aloud to yourself, or better yet find someone to read it to you. Many things that seemed all right as written may now sound awkward or stilted. The spoken word, even in formal situations, is much less formal than the written word. There is less importance put on sentence structure and less attention called to slight errors in grammar. Slang terms are used more often in speaking than in writing, although you should be careful with slang because it can become quickly outdated.

The feelings and style of delivery should be apparent from the content of the scene. This means that you should rarely have to include stage directions telling how the line is to be delivered. If the scene is well written and if the mood or atmosphere is conveyed through the sense of the action, you can be fairly certain that the lines will be delivered effectively.

Also, keep in mind that one speech usually leads directly into the next without abrupt changes. Almost every line is a cue line for another character, so the character has to have a reason for responding.

ACTIVITIES

1. Record three different conversations among people of different backgrounds. What are the differences in the way they spoke, in the subject matter, in the language and in the direction of the conversation?

2. Write an analysis of a participant in one of these conversations. Include what you know as well as what you can assume. On what basis did you make the assumptions?

3. Record another conversation of approximately three minutes. On the basis of your impression of the participants, extend the conversation another two minutes.

4. Make a recorded conversation more effective through selectivity.

5. Take the same conversation and, using all the techniques you can, make it more interesting and more dramatically effective.

6. Choose a scene from a published play. Slightly change the direction and the outcome by altering the dialog.

7. Write a short section of dialog in which one or more of the participants speaks with an accent.

8. Previously, you developed a central character and placed him or her in some scenes. Choose one of these scenes and rewrite the dialog to make it more effective.

9. Write a short scene in which one or more traits of your central character are revealed largely through action, rather than

through dialog.

10. Write dialog for a scene in which the central character you have developed is having a quarrel with another character.

11. Write another scene in which your central character is feeling happiness, frustration or anxiety.

CHAPTER 11

Planning and Revising

Often, it takes time for an idea to germinate and to grow. Most writers at least have an idea about plot, theme or characters before they start. Some prefer to do an intricate scenario or synopsis, others a minimal outline and some only notes. It doesn't matter how much you do before starting the script. What matters is that it works.

An advantage of detailed planning is that the writing may get started and progress faster than if you've done minimal planning. Another advantage is that a detailed plan may show the strengths and weaknesses. You can see, for instance, if the relationships are logical and if the characters have strong enough differences to provide conflict.

A disadvantage is that the play may become too rigid.

DETAILS OF THE PLANNING

It's a good idea to state your theme clearly so that you know where you're going with the play. If you are unable to write in no more than a couple of sentences what the play is "about," you probably don't have a clear idea yourself. You don't have to have a theme immediately, but you should before long to keep the play from rambling. In one of my plays discussed earlier, Rita refuses to give up unrealistic dreams. The theme is: You have to learn to accept responsibility for your actions. For another of my plays, *To Ride a Wild Pony*, I explore the issue of dependence. One of the two people has quit college to raise the other's son. The first thus becomes totally dependent on the second for the necessities of life. The idea is that life rarely is satisfactory if one person is completely dependent upon another. The theme then might be stated as: Each person needs a degree of freedom, of independence. I actually started this play with that idea in mind, whereas others I've begun are based on situations or characters.

As you saw earlier, one of the first steps in planning the script is the character analysis. If you don't have much experience as a playwright, it's a good idea to go through all the questions on paper. Later you may find it enough to think them through, or even sometimes let the character develop as you go along, sort of like the character interview.

Another part of the planning may be the setting. But this doesn't necessarily mean working it out in detail. It may be enough for you to know that the action occurs in a middle-class apartment in the Hillcrest area of San Diego. Yet such a setting is important because it may become almost a character itself. For instance, in Franz Werfel's play *The Goat Song*, there is a mysterious building on the farm, a building that nobody wants to discuss. It becomes pervasive, ominous, until it is discovered that the building has concealed since birth the beastlike son of the wealthy landowner Stevan Milic.

In Tennessee Williams' *The Glass Menagerie*, the apartment where Laura, her mother and her brother live is a dark, depressing place that symbolizes the type of lives the characters lead.

In the matter of planning a setting, decide what works best for you. If you're the type of person who can more easily visualize your characters in a detailed setting, by all means work it out. But remember the scene designer, working with the director and other designers, probably will have different ideas. However, he or she certainly will want to maintain the mood and sense of place you envisioned, if it is particularly important.

In all probability, when you write dialog and scenes, you won't want to slow down the dialog to write stage directions or details of setting. You can put them in later. It's more important to keep the writing fluid. One important thing to figure out, however, is where your characters have been before entering and where they are going when they leave. Why are they entering or exiting? They have to have reasons for what they do; they can't just suddenly appear out of nowhere or conversely wander off into a nebulous somewhere.

EXPOSITION

You need to take great care in planning how to include the exposition. This, as you learned, is anything the audience needs to know about prior events, given circumstances (conditions of the time), personality traits, the current situation or relationship among characters, in order to have an understanding of the action.

Most often you can work the exposition into the scene bit by bit so that it's less obtrusive than in *Fashion*, for instance.

There are two types of exposition. The first involves background material. The second type is related to the changing situations and the constant revelation of character.

Background exposition deals with the opening situation of the play. What are the general economic conditions not only of the characters but also of the world in which they exist? Where does the action take place? Is there anything the audience needs to know about that location? Is it a desolate farmhouse, easily accessible to pranksters or thieves? Is it a slum area where stepping outside can mean being assaulted and beaten? What is the condition of the city or the country where the action takes place? What are the prevailing attitudes of the population? What are the feelings of the time? How do the central and secondary characters' feelings mesh with what their country or the world in general believes?

If the play takes place in another time or location, or even in a world totally different than the one we live in, what are the prevailing conditions? Are the natural laws the same as would be expected in our own world or in our own time? Setting forth exposition of this sort is establishing a frame of reference that the audience will then accept. Yet, as you learned, it has to remain consistent, unless, of course, something like a worldwide disaster changes it.

What about the characters themselves? What sort of lives have they led? What are their economic and social conditions? What type of people are they? Of course, this is the sort of thing you figure out when you do your character analysis where you learn much more than the audience ever needs to know. However, you do need to determine what is important for the audience to grasp, and how you can bring this across.

Progressive Exposition continues throughout the play and is related to the unraveling of the plot and the revelation of character. Certain feelings a character has may not be so important for the audience to know at the beginning of the play as they are later. To understand a character's reaction, the audience must know his or her feelings at the present time and the reason for these feelings. It is important to know, for instance, at the beginning of my *To Ride a Wild Pony* that Dennis gave up college and his dreams of becoming an artist in order to be financially secure, to have a home he needn't worry about losing, to have all his material needs met.

Only later is it important to discover the reason for this, that he'd been kicked out of his aunt's house (or thought he had been) and as a fourteen-year-old had had to survive on his own for several months in New York City.

In figuring out the exposition, you also need to figure out what has caused the inciting incident? Why has an event occurred that puts the protagonist into conflict? Dennis, for instance, realizes life has passed him by, and he's accomplished nothing. He's quit painting, he's never had a full-time job (other than taking care of a child), and he's feeling a strong sense of mortality because the man who's provided the financial security has had a serious heart attack. This is enough to make Dennis realize that if he doesn't do something with his life now, he never will.

How will the protagonist react differently to what has happened than will anyone else? Why? Dennis reacts differently because he has a lot of drive that he's managed to suppress. He is very talented, though he's never given himself adequate chance to explore this. If he were totally unambitious or if he came from a different background, rather than one in which he literally had to fight each day to survive, he probably would care deeply that his friend has had the heart attack, but it wouldn't change the way he continues to live.

Since exposition is such an important part of understanding the play, you may want to write down as much of it as you can figure out before beginning the script. That way you can be sure everything the audience needs to know is included. Of course, as the scenes and the action progress, other things will come up that you hadn't thought of earlier. Sometimes this means going back and revising scenes to include the information.

There are many techniques for presenting exposition (some of which you encountered earlier):

1. Straightforward and direct using the device of a narrator, such as the Stage Manager's monolog in *Our Town* and Hamlet's soliloquies. This technique works in part because of the

type of play this is, because it jumps from one time to another so quickly. The stage manager becomes the "bridge" between scenes. He provides coherence and is the unifying force. Generally, however, you should not need a narrator. If you do, you may have chosen the wrong medium to tell your story. It might work better as a novel or novelette. That isn't to say you should avoid a narrator altogether, but you certainly should question why you need one.

2. Through the flashback, used for example, in *Death of a Salesman*. This is a means of "showing" past events that have a direct bearing on the play. This can be effective since the action of a play, unlike a novel, occurs in a continuing present time. That is, even when we travel backward in time to pick up a scene of this sort, we restart the clock, so to speak, so that the audience "sees" the scene as it is occurring. Like the use of a narrator, flashbacks can be effective, but it generally is good to use them sparingly or they can become confusing. Often, there really isn't the need for them. They work well in Miller's play because they show the past colored by Willy's memories, rather than showing it more objectively. One cardinal rule: Never place a flashback inside a flashback.

3. Through conflict, as you saw in the "John and Marsha" scene in Chapter 9 and in the scene from *The Importance of Being Earnest*. It's much more interesting this way than having the audience listen to straight narration. It also moves the plot forward since the conflict usually has its base in the central problem.

4. Through characters talking about another person. An example would be the scene in *The Fantasticks* where the fathers of Matt and Luisa are singing about knowing how vegetables will turn out once you plant them, but the difficulty in knowing how children will turn out, or in *The Miracle Worker* where the family talks about how illness caused Helen Keller to lose her sight and hearing.

These scenes are valid because they provide information on conditions and problems. But as you know, the best way to show character is to see and hear the person, not to have others merely talk about him or her.

5. Through such devices as meetings, partings, or reunions where people always tend to reminisce.

6. Through other special occasions, such as memorial services or retirements, where once again people reminisce about knowing someone and the experiences they've had together.

7. By introductions, such as at a party, where you might introduce two people and tell a little about each so the two have something to talk about or maybe a common ground. For example, a sometimes actor I know, at lunchtime today, came into the coffee shop where he works part-time and saw my friend and me and another friend. Although he himself had to leave, he told the friend, "You should talk to Marsh, he's a writer." He said to me, "You should get to know Gayle because she's an actress and writer."

Of course, the two of us found we had a lot in common and spent an hour talking, vowing to keep in touch.

8. Through touches of anger or irritation. "Damnit, Charlie, this is the second time today I've had to clean up your dishes. Half the time you don't put your clothes in the hamper or hang up your jacket."

9. Through scenery, lighting, costuming, props and makeup. The setting, unless it's abstract, shows the location and often the circumstances of the characters. The lighting and costuming can give clues to the season and the time of day, for instance.

If you rank the expository material in the order by which it needs to be known or as it becomes more important, you can weave it in gradually. What the audience needs to know, for instance, at the opening of the second act may not have been necessary for them to know at the beginning of the play.

You can also divide the exposition into various types and then list what the audience needs to know, and when they need to know it. For instance:

I. General conditions of the character's world.

    A. A backward civilization, similar to that of the late nineteenth century.

    B. Fifty years or so after a nuclear holocaust.

    C. Few modern conveniences.

    D. Gaslights, travel by horse and buggy.

    E. Scant population.

II. Government

    A. There are governors (dictators) who rule each province; they have near absolute power.

    B. Each province is pretty much a police state.

    C. The governors are the only men, besides actors, who take the formula. Usually, they alter themselves to become similar to people throughout history that they admire.

II. The protagonist's world.

    A. People are compelled to become actors, even though they may not want to.

    B. Actors are forbidden to have contact with their old lives and families.

    C. Actors take a formula which wreaks havoc with their bodies.

        1. Developed and defined years earlier by a man named Parsons Dowd.

        2. Alters the actors' genetic makeup so that they actually become the characters they portray.

        3. An antidote changes them back.

        4. They die young.

    D. Actors take names of performers throughout history; they no longer use their birth names.

This is the sort of thing you need to determine, and these are the sorts of things the playwright Zachary Thomas would have figured out before beginning his play *Death by Stages* (based on one of my stories).

Here is a scene from near the end of the first act. As you might gather, Colley Cibber has a body that for some reason will not alter when he takes the formula, yet he is one of the few people who really wants to be an actor.

In a scene preceding this one, Marilyn Monroe took a potion to try to regain her own body after playing the role of the maid in O'Neill's *Long Day's Journey Into Night*. The potion does not work, and so she remains the character. She rushes from the theatre in hysterics.

The actors, as is customary after each performance, go to dinner at an inn. The two central characters in *Death by Stages* are Will Shakespeare and Nell Gwynn.

(Everyone is seated at a large round table in an Elizabethan-style inn as WILL and NELL enter.)

WILL: I see you haven't been served yet.

CHEKHOV: Any word about Marilyn? *(HELEN HAYES and SARAH BERNHARDT scoot their chairs around to make room. WILL holds a chair for NELL. She sits down and so does WILL.)*

ROBESON: Is Marilyn all right?

NELL: It would seem so. But we can't be certain.

CHEKHOV: What do you mean?

NELL: She wasn't at her lodging.

HELEN: It's a darned shame.

CHEKHOV: How could this happen? The formulas have worked for a hundred years.

ROBESON: Have they?

GARRICK: I don't follow your meaning. I think their development was a wonder. A boon for all of us who would tread the boards.

BERNHARDT: Perhaps. Nevertheless, we have little to look forward to beyond the gaslights and makeup.

CHEKHOV: I, for one, think the man who developed the formulas should rot in hell through all eternity for what he's done.

WILL: Parsons Dowd?

CHEKHOV: That's right.

GARRICK: I disagree. If it weren't for the theatre, my mum and my brothers and sister would be turned out in the streets by now.

CHEKHOV: There is that. But it seems to me —

ROBESON: It seems to me that we have big trouble on our hands. *(He looks from face to face.)* Things have gone strangely awry the past few days.

HELEN: The formula's gone bad, is that what you mean?

ROBESON: I for one don't think it's the formulas.

CHEKHOV: Nor I.

BERNHARDT: Are you implying it's deliberate? That someone's behind it?

184

CHEKHOV: Figure it out for yourself. Never in the history of the theatre has this thing happened.

ROBESON: Or so we're led to believe.

WILL: You're right. There's no way of knowing.

ROBESON: I suspect someone's deliberately altering the formulas.

WILL: But who? And for what purpose?

BERNHARDT: I can think of one person.

WILL: I've had my suspicions too. But I have nothing to base them on.

GARRICK: Of course, you mean Cibber. *(He looks WILL straight in the eyes, a seeming taunt behind the words.)*

WILL: *(Irritated)* Because he can't alter his body?

GIELGUD: I understand Richard Burbage took the poison. Well before his years.

WAYNE: Don't worry none, laddie. Your time ain't coming for awhile yet. *(GIELGUD gives WAYNE a dirty look.)*

CHEKHOV: So I assume that most of us suspect some sort of foul play. *(The others murmur assent.)* So what are we going to do?

WILL: *(Glancing at NELL)* Nell, are you all right?

NELL: As much as anyone can be in times like these. What's to be done?

ROBESON: You said you couldn't find Marilyn. Where do you suppose she's gone?

WILL: *(Pulling a note from his pocket)* This is all she said. *(He hands the paper to HELEN who glances at it and then passes it around the table.)* What about it, Nell? Did she say anything before she ran off? Anything that would give you a clue?

NELL: No. *(She frowns.)* Yes. Yes, she did. She shouted something to Smitley about getting the guilty person.

WILL: What did she mean? Do you think she suspected someone?

NELL: *(Shaking her head)* Who could she have suspected? Who would do such a terrible thing?

CHEKHOV: Who do you think? You get two guesses and the second doesn't count.

BERNHARDT: Cibber, of course. Who else?

WILL: I can't imagine he'd do such a terrible thing. And what would be his motive?

GARRICK: Jealousy. He wants to be one of us and can't be. Isn't that plain?

NELL: But to do something so extreme. No, I never liked the man, but I don't see how he'd be capable of doing something like this.

ROBESON: Where is he tonight, by the way? It's not like him to miss out on dinner. *(GARRICK snickers.)*

ROBESON: *(Giving him a piercing look)* I didn't mean to imply that the man shouldn't eat.

GARRICK: Isn't it obvious that's who Marilyn went to see?

WILL: But why?

BERNHARDT: Maybe Garrick's right. I've always thought it a little strange that Cibber never could change. Especially when he wants to be one of us.

CHEKHOV: They tell me that a lot of youngsters used to be stagestruck. They dreamed of careers in the theatre. In fact, the man whose name I took wrote lessons for this sort of person. I think Cibber's like one of those youngsters. The theatre means so much to him that I ... well, I just can't see him doing anything to hurt it or anyone in it.

WAYNE: It's interesting. Some of us had other ambitions, would give anything not to be actors. And then someone like Cibber is just the opposite. He apparently would sell his soul to be able to change.

HELEN: Didn't there used to be a saying about the grass always being greener somewhere else?

GIELGUD : I like the company and all. But if I could, I'd rather be doing other work. This wouldn't have been my choice.

WAYNE: And what would you rather be doing? Raising brats or raising chickens?

GARRICK: I've always been interested in carpentry and in building.

WAYNE: *(Laughing derisively)* Do you liken yourself to our Lord?

WILL: Leave the boy be. Most of us have other dreams, lives that might have been.

ROBESON: These are serious times. We shouldn't bicker but must stick together.

186

THE STORY LINE

Another thing you can plan is the plot. There are several ways of doing this. One is the outline.

For each division you include the characters, the location, the time and a description of the action. The emotional content might also be included. For example:

I. Act I

   A. Scene 1

      1. Characters — Jim and Helen Peters.

      2. Location — The Peters' living room.

      3. Time — Friday at 6 p.m.

      4. Progression of the action.

         a. Helen has just learned of her brother's death.

         b. Jim comes home from work.

         c. Jim and Helen consider the advisability of visiting the town where her brother lived to investigate his death.

         d. Helen becomes hysterical when Jim objects to going.

A second method is to write out in paragraph form an abbreviated version of what will transpire:

> The scene occurs in the Peters' living room in Columbus, Ohio. It is early Friday evening. As the action begins, Helen is talking on the phone. Her sister has called to tell her of their brother's death. As she hangs up the phone, Jim comes home from work. Barely able to speak, she tells him that Tom was shot and killed on a beach in La Jolla, California. Because Jim has been out of work, they have little money. Helen wants to go to the town where her brother lived to investigate his death. Jim is sympathetic but reminds her they have little money. She becomes hysterical.

Another way to plan the scenes is to write a skeletal version of the script, using actual dialog.

It also doesn't matter whether or not you start at the

187

beginning and go straight through. You may want to write particular scenes first.

Somewhere along the way try to come up with a title which says something important, revealing or intriguing.

No matter which type of outline you use, you should include such things as the prevailing mood, the situation, the dramatic question, the given circumstances, and a description of the characters and how they fit into the play as a whole.

PROPORTIONING THE ACTS

You need a balance, neither revealing too much or too little in each act. Too little will cause the play to lag; too much will leave nothing to maintain interest in succeeding acts. By the end of the first act the audience should have all the background material necessary for an understanding of the play. For instance, in Ibsen's *An Enemy of the People*, we know by the end of the first act how important the baths are to the economic survival of the town, and we can see the type of person Dr. Stockmann is. We know that he will try to have the baths shut down, and we know, because they disagree about so many things, his brother, the burgomaster, will oppose him. In other words, we see the entire conflict shaping up and we understand what is likely to happen and why. There generally should be only character and plot revelation (or exposition) after this point.

In a three-act play, each of the first two acts should end on a high point to build audience anticipation for what is to follow. The first act of *West Side Story* ends just after Bernardo of the Sharks stabs Riff of the Jets. Then Tony jumps forward and stabs Bernardo. Police whistles sound. The gangs disappear, except for Tony and a girl named Anybodys. She tries to pull him offstage. He finally realizes the danger he's in and escapes as a police searchlight cuts across the stage, a dramatic and emotional first act ending.

If the climax of the play is too early, remaining scenes can't be very interesting. If it occurs too late, the audience may feel cheated in not seeing the results of the resolution. Usually, the climax should come toward the middle of the third act.

REVISING THE PLAY

You may have two, four, five or ten drafts before you are satisfied. This can include expanding, rearranging or cutting. You may find that new scenes or dialog are needed for clarity. Perhaps a scene just does not come across as you intended when you first wrote the material and it has to be changed.

You shouldn't hesitate to throw out a scene that doesn't quite say what was intended or that isn't important.

Much of the work of revising is in tightening scenes and dialog. Sometimes you can eliminate as much as half of what you have written because it is repetitive or lacks direction.

During the revision you can plan the setting exactly the way you want it. Now is the time to consider it practically. Generally, it's better to have as few changes of scenery as possible due to the expense, backstage storage and the time required for scenery shifts.

You don't have to be an expert designer, but you should know the elements of scenery construction and what works and what doesn't. If you at least are acquainted with design and construction, you will be better able to write a play that can be practicably executed.

Another consideration in revising the script is stage directions. Generally, the fewer the better. It's pointless to include in great detail how the setting should be used and how the actors should move and react. Directors want to have their own say about what is to be done.

I've always found that it helps to read the dialog aloud. I can better tell then if it has the ring of authenticity or not. Does it sound like everyday conversation (as each of my characters would speak it), or is it too stilted?

It can be helpful to hear someone else read the play aloud. Of course, it's good to have readers who have some experience as actors or in doing this sort of thing. Now you can listen more objectively; you can judge better how the dialog falls on the ear, and if you've written the scene clearly enough that the readers have no trouble interpreting it.

Does it contain tongue twisters, other words and phrases that make the readers stumble repeatedly? Do the characters come across as you intended them? Certainly, the readers will add their own backgrounds and interpretations to the roles, but this should come across as an added dimension, rather than as something totally alien to what you wanted.

Often after hearing your play read, you will find you need to sharpen dialog or character, to build scenes more effectively, to make the exposition and the characters' intentions clearer.

One other bit of advice: Often when you work intensely with a particular project, because you are so close to it, you lose your objectivity. You find that you can't tell if a scene is good or bad, whether a character comes across the way you want or not.

Even if you feel this isn't happening and you can judge the play fairly, still put it away for a week or two weeks or a month. Then you can come back to it with a fresh perspective. I guarantee that you'll see things that can be improved — even including typos and other minor errors.

ACTIVITIES

1. Using the central character and the situations you previously wrote, develop a plan for a full-length play, using whatever form of outline you find works well for you.

2. Make a list of the background exposition that is necessary. Rank it in order of importance.

3. Determine the type of setting you want to use.

4. Write a scene in which you include all *necessary* stage directions.

5. Determine any special conditions of time, place, or general attitude that will affect the progression of your play.

6. Write a scene in which you include background exposition.

7. Take a scene you have written and revise it as completely to your satisfaction as you can.

190

CHAPTER 12

Producing and Publishing

After your play is finished, the important thing is to have it produced or published. If you've defined the type of audience for whom you are writing, you should have little trouble choosing a specific market.

You often have a better chance of having your play presented in a theatre with which you are affiliated, or at least where you know people. There are several options you might try even in a theatre such as this before seeking a full production.

One is a cold or non-rehearsed reading. If you or others at the theatre can help you round up enough actors willing to give the play a reading, you will have the opportunity of hearing the dialog actually presented by experienced people.

Also there are various types of playwriting workshops you might try, some connected with theatres, others operating on their own. Here the process is similar in that members (often with at least some experience as actors) give the play a cold reading. Certainly, a rehearsed presentation would be more helpful, but many actors do give excellent cold readings. The Dramatists Guild also lists various playwriting workshops held in cities across the country.

Often at the end of such readings — whether at a theatre or with an independent group — there is a discussion of the play's merits, of its positive aspects and of those parts workshop participants feel need to be improved.

Some workshops, of course, are better than others. Those that are most helpful have members who give honest critiques with the intention of helping, rather than tearing down. However, do use caution. I've seen many workshops in which the members seem more interested in showing off how intelligent they are and how stupid or inept the playwright is than in being helpful.

Particularly, if you live in a fair-sized or large city, you should have no trouble finding workshops. For instance, in San Diego, there is a place called the Writing Center that has workshops. The public library keeps a list of writer's organizations, which, if they can't help you themselves, often can put you in touch with people who can. Some cities, like Los Angeles and San Diego, have publications listing workshops or even theatres willing to consider scripts for cold readings.

Many theatres across the country have play development programs. Some provide the means for cold readings. Many go even further in offering staged readings to plays they feel have the potential for success. Often staged readings lead to full productions, either at the same theatre or at different theatres.

Staged readings are just what the name implies. The actors rehearse the play at least a few times but read from the books. This gives a better idea of how the play will move because it includes physical action, though, of course, it will not have a setting developed just for the play, and some of the physical activities and use of props will be limited. However, it does give the writer a better idea of how the script will play in a full production.

Staged readings are given before an audience, so you can judge their reaction. Often, theatres or playwrights themselves prepare questionnaires to hand out to the audience asking what they liked or disliked about the play. Often the questions are much more specific: What do you think was the theme of this play? Did you have any trouble following the action? If so, in which scene? And so on.

Next, of course, is to have the play produced. Often during rehearsals, you will be required to be there to rewrite anything that the director, in particular, or sometimes the actors feel is unworkable — an awkward or stilted phrase, an unclear scene, action that doesn't build. In a way, this is a sort of tryout period. Even after this first production, you are almost certain to find that you need some rewriting. Things come across differently when performed before a theatre audience than they do when you read them to yourself or even have a cold or staged reading.

There are some professional markets — producers and publishers — who want only previously produced plays submitted to them. Generally, a producer will take only "run-of-the-play" rights. You should beware of selling a script to a market, particularly a producer, who wants to buy all the rights since you could lose a great deal of money that way. Particularly, if you sell

192

the play to a publisher, it's generally not a good idea to sell it outright. Instead, you'll want royalties.

PREPARING THE MANUSCRIPT

The play should look readable and professional. A producer or publisher may think that if you didn't know enough or care enough to present the manuscript correctly, the play can't be very good.

You should use white sixteen or twenty pound paper that is letter size. Don't use erasable paper as it smudges easily. The best thing is to submit good quality photocopies. That way you can hang on to the original, which won't be damaged or lost.

Use either standard elite or pica type. Stay away from script or exotic styles, and stay away from non-letter quality or dot matrix printers. Your margins should be one inch on the right side, one and a half inches at the left, and an inch and a quarter at the top and bottom.

Page numbers should appear in the upper right hand corner of each page. They should include three things: the act number, the scene number, and the page number. For example, the second page of Act I, Scene 1, would be written: I-1-2. The final number begins again with "1" at the beginning of each act: II-1-1.

Several prefatory pages should be included. The first is the title page, which contains the name of the play in capital letters and is centered about a third of the way down the page. The title is underlined. Centered under the title and three spaces down should be the byline with your name in capital letters. The copyright notice (see below) appears at the bottom, left-hand side of the page.

After the title page is an unnumbered page listing the cast of characters and, if desired, an identification of each. For example:

CAST OF CHARACTERS

JOSEPH SMITH, 39, father of JIM and SUSIE SMITH

HELEN SMITH, 34, wife of JOSEPH

ROBERT BROWN, 65, grandfather of JIM and SUSIE

On the same page as the cast of characters you can include the time and place of the action. If there isn't enough room, it can be at the top of the next page. For example:

> *The action occurs during a weekend in November on the Smith farm in New Hampshire. The time is the present.*

The next page, also unnumbered, contains the synopsis of scenes and a description of the setting:

SYNOPSIS OF SCENES

ACT I

The Smith farmhouse. About 2 p.m. Friday.

ACT II

The same. Saturday evening.

ACT III

The same. Saturday evening.

SETTING: The Smith home is a typical farmhouse, constructed in the early twentieth century. The living room contains a few hard-backed chairs, a sofa, and a fireplace. There are a few occasional tables and a painting or two on each of the walls. The floor is covered with a braided rug. One doorway leads to the kitchen; the other leads upstairs. There is a window overlooking the grove, a wooded area with tall shade trees.

Before each act is another unnumbered page, which gives the title of the play, underlined, in caps and centered. Three spaces under the title appears the act designation, e.g, Act II, also centered and in caps.

For scripts submitted to producers or agents, on the dialog pages, the characters' names, before their dialog and in the stage directions, should be in capital letters and approximately four inches from the left-hand margin. All stage directions, except those of a word or two, should also be indented about four inches, in parenthesis, and single spaced. Dialog begins at the left margin. Everything is single-spaced except that there should be a double space between the final stage direction or dialog of one character and that of the next character. Directions of only a few words can appear in parentheses within the lines of dialog. When a character makes the first appearance, the description should be given in parentheses in the same manner as a stage direction. Dialog is never paragraphed, and each scene and act

194

should be ended as follows: END OF ACT II, SCENE 1. Such a notice should be triple-spaced and centered below the last line of the dialog or stage direction. The words, THE END, should appear at the conclusion of the play.

```
                          SARAH
                          (Talking on the telephone.)
          I don't know what I'm going to do.  I just can't take it.
          Twenty-four hours a day and no relief.  (Pause.)  Well,
          maybe sometimes on Friday night when Jim comes down.   Then I
          can go quilting or out to dinner.  (Pause.)  Well, your
          phone bill is going to be awful high, Cathy.  I'll call
          Saturday night when your Dad comes.  He can talk too.

                                   (GRANDMA PAULSEN enters from the
                                   living room.  A tall, thin woman
                                   of eighty-six, she is dressed in a
                                   homemade, flower-print dress, which
                                   fits loosely and comes down a few
                                   inches below her knees.  A faded
                                   apron is tied around her waist.
                                   She wears heavy brown stockings and
                                   black oxfords.  Slightly stooped,
                                   she walks very slowly.  She wears
                                   wire-rimmed glasses and her eyes
                                   are always sad.  She is muttering
                                   as she enters.)

                          GRANDMA PAULSEN
          Well, are you talking to her again?  She sure does know how
          to waste money.

                          SARAH
                          (She glances toward GRANDMA PAULSEN
                          before speaking again.)
          Well, I guess I better get supper now.  We can talk later.
          Chin up.  'Bye.  (Pause.)  I love you too.

                          GRANDMA PAULSEN
                          (She sits at the kitchen table.)
          Let's have that roast beef tonight that the Fosters gave
          you.  And maybe some mixed vegetables and canned pears.  And
          don't cook as much as you did at noon.  You know I just
          can't eat much anymore, and Pop doesn't either.  (Pause.)
          And you have to watch your weight, you know.  (Pause.)  I
          think we could use some coal on that furnace.

                          SARAH
                          (She crosses to the cellar door.)
          Okay, Mom, but it seems pretty warm in here to me.

                          GRANDMA PAULSEN
          Well, I'm cold.  Maybe if you fix me a cup of coffee, it
          would help.  You'd better check the furnace, though, just to
          be sure.
```

For some publishers, the format is different, with the characters' names appearing on the left, followed by a colon before the dialog. Here is a sample page prepared in this manner. Of course, you might want to check with the publisher as to the desired format before submitting a script. However, here is what a page of a script that you submit to a publisher might look like. Notice the difference in the page heading. Here the playwright's name is given on the left, key words from the title and the actual manuscript page number on the left.

CAST OF CHARACTERS

WILL, as ancient as a newborn babe
LARRY, about 35

Setting: The action takes place in Larry's apartment in La Jolla, California, a rich suburb of San Diego.

At Rise: We hear the strands of an English madrigal over the sound system. It fades, and we seem to be dropped right into the middle of a highly emotional scene occurring in LARRY'S apartment.

WILL: I cannot recall! If thou canst help, prithee do.

LARRY: One day it will be clear. Just trust me.

WILL: Clear? That's plain nonsense! A tale told by a
               moron. Full of noise and anger. Meaning not a
               blessed thing! (He begins breathing unevenly as
               if about to break into sobs.)

LARRY: For heaven's sake, calm down.

WILL: Full of fury and clamor! Sound and anger. Noise
               and fury. A tale told by an idiot. Full of sound
               and fury, signifying nothing!

LARRY: You have to accept that yours is one of the
               greatest minds--

WILL: (Pounding his fist on whatever surface is
               available) But I don't know who I am.

LARRY: (Sighs) I'm a scientist, right? I clone things.

WILL: Jumping frogs and creeping rats.

LARRY: Yes, at first. Then I discovered I could
               revitalize cells after death, particularly bone
               cells, which like all others contain the imprint
               of the entire being. (Pause) I have a passion
               for theatre. And for me one playwright stands out
               above all others. William Shakespeare.

WILL: I swear, as long as men can breathe and eyes can
               see, I'll never understand your riddles.

LARRY: You did it again.

WILL: What?

The following then is how it might look in print.

```
1                    The Study of Shakespeare
2
3    CAST:  WILL, as ancient as a newborn babe; LARRY, about 35.
4    SETTING:   The action takes place in Larry's apartment in La Jolla,
5         California, a rich suburb of San Diego.
6    AT RISE:   We hear the strains of an English madrigal over the
7         sound system. It fades, and we seem to be dropped right into
8         the middle of a highly emotional scene occurring in LARRY's
9         apartment.
10
11   WILL:   I cannot recall! If thou canst help, prithee do.
12   LARRY:   One day it will be clear. Just trust me.
13   WILL:   Clear? That's plain nonsense! A tale told by a moron.
14        Full of noise and anger. Meaning not a blessed thing! (He
15        begins breathing unevenly as if about to break into sobs.)
16   LARRY:   For heaven's sake, calm down.
17   WILL:   Full of fury and clamor! Sound and anger. Noise and
18        fury. A tale told by an idiot. Full of sound and fury,
19        signifying nothing!
20   LARRY:   You have to accept that yours is one of the greatest
21        minds —
22   WILL:   (Pounding his fist on whatever surface is available) But I
23        don't know who I am.
24   LARRY:   (Sighs.) I'm a scientist, right? I clone things.
25   WILL:   Jumping frogs and creeping rats.
26   LARRY:   Yes, at first. Then I discovered I could revitalize
27        cells after death, particularly bone cells, which like all
28        others contain the imprint of the entire being. (Pause) I
29        have a passion for theatre. And for me one playwright
30        stands out above all others. William Shakespeare.
31   WILL:   I swear, as long as men can breathe and eyes can see,
32        I'll never understand your riddles.
33   LARRY:   You did it again.
34   WILL:   What?
35   LARRY:   Shakespeare's sonnet. Number eighteen, I think.
```

As soon as your play is written, it is protected as "Common Law Literary Property." This form of copyright lasts as long as the work is unpublished or until Statutory Copyright is secured. The latter applies only to unpublished forms such as musical compositions, plays, art works and some other specialized forms.

If you are sending the play to an unfamiliar market, you may want to include a copyright line such as: Copyright 1999, YOUR NAME. In order to prove ownership of a script, some playwrights mail themselves a copy that they leave unopened.

If you do want to secure a Statutory Copyright, you can register a claim with the Federal Copyright Office. A form can be obtained by writing to: Copyright Office, The Library of Congress, Washington, DC 20559. Request a copy of "Form PA," which is the proper one for copyrighting plays. After you receive your form, fill it out and return it with a copy of your script and the required fee.

Before copyrighting your play, be sure it is revised as completely as possible, and you are ready to send it out. The reason is that the copyright notice lists the year in which the play was registered, and it may appear outdated before you ever submit it to a theatre. On the other hand, some professional producers won't look at a play that isn't copyrighted.

The next step is to prepare it for mailing. The script should be secured at the left side in some sort of binder. It should then be sent in a manila envelope. Be sure to enclose a self-addressed envelope and return postage in the event your script is to be returned.

Any manuscripts can be mailed at a special fourth class rate (often called book rate), which is considerably less expensive than mailing your submissions at first class rates. First class or priority mail does receive preferential treatment and usually arrives at its destination much more quickly, so it probably is worth the added expense.

One of the most important considerations is choosing an appropriate market. You can submit plays to producers, contests, professional theatre companies, educational theatres, community theatres, various summer theatres and publishers. There are many ways of investigating markets. One of the best is to find any theatres in your area which would be willing to produce original plays. You may be surprised to learn that they include high schools, colleges, children's theatre groups, community theatres and regional professional theatres.

You can find listings in such books as *Dramatists Sourcebook*, published each August by the Theatre Communications Group in New York, and in *The Playwright's Companion*, published yearly by Feedback Theatrebooks of New York. Each has a fairly comprehensive list of producers, publishers, and agents as well as listing various playwriting prizes, festivals, conferences and workshops for playwrights.

Another source is *Writer's Market*, published annually, by Writer's Digest Books. Because this book lists various types of writing markets, the listing that pertains to plays is of necessity smaller than the other listings. Yet it does contain the names of both publishers and producers.

Some of the writing magazines also devote space to playwrights' markets. One of the best for this is *The Writer*.

It also helps to join the Dramatists Guild as an associate member. The organization publishes both newsletters and quarterly journals which give many listings of theatres looking for scripts. The address is 234 W. 44th St., New York, NY 10036.

There are a variety of organizations, including arts councils in many states, that provide grants or aid to playwrights. Some of these also offer an opportunity for production. Learn as much as you can about the theatres where you may submit your work. Plays often are produced through having the right contacts with producers, directors or actors. Many times, if they know a new playwright, they will be more willing to give him or her a chance.

A final word about marketing. When submitting to most theatres and even play publishers, you don't need an agent. Also, most agents won't handle the work of a new playwright, and many of those who say they will often charge a reading fee of up to several hundred dollars. Some reputable agents charge such fees as a means of justifying time spent in working with new writers. However, beware; there are many unscrupulous, so-called agents who do little more than take your money and offer an often useless critique of your work.

An agent's major function is to handle some of the business details and the matter of contracts. If you do want to contact an agent, you can get a list of those who handle plays by writing to the Society of Authors' Representatives, Inc., 10 Astor Pl., 3rd Floor, New York, New York 10036, or the Authors Guild of America, 234 W. 34th St., New York, New York 10003. *Poets & Writer's Magazine* publishes a book called *Literary Agents: A Writer's Guide*. The Dramatist Guild also lists agents who handle plays.

SELECTED BIBLIOGRAPHY

Archer, William. Play-Making: *A Manual of Craftsmanship.* New York: Dodd, Mead & Co., 1928.

Baker, George Pierce. *Dramatic Technique.* Boston: Houghton Mifflin Co., 1919.

Busfield, Roger M., Jr. *The Playwright's Art.* New York: Harper & Brothers, 1958.

Chapman, Gerald. *Teaching Young Playwrights.* Portsmouth, New Hampshire: Heinemann, 1991.

Egri, Lajos. *The Art of Dramatic Writing.* New York: Simon and Schuster, 1946.

Ervine, St. John. *How to Write a Play.* New York: The Macmillan Co., 1928.

Frome, Shelly. *Playwriting: A Complete Guide to Creating Theater.* Jefferson, North Carolina: McFarland & Company, Inc., Publishers, 1990.

George, Kathleen E. *Playwriting: The First Workshop.* Boston: Focal Press, 1994.

Grenbanier, Bernard. *Playwriting.* New York: Thomas Y. Crowell Co., 1961.

Howard, Louise, and Jeron Criswell. *How Your Play Can Crash Broadway.* New York: Howard and Criswell, 1939.

Hull, Raymond. *How to Write a Play.* Cincinnati: Writer's Digest Books, 1983.

Kerr, Walter. *How Not to Write a Play.* New York: Simon and Schuster, 1955.

Langner, Lawrence. *The Play's the Thing.* New York: G. P. Putnam's Sons, 1960.

Lawson, John Howard. *Theory and Technique of Playwriting.* Copyright, 1936, G. P. Putnam's Sons; rpt. New York: Hill and Wang, 1960.

Matthews, Brander, ed. *Papers on Playmaking.* New York: Hill and Wang, 1957.

Niggli, Josefina. *New Pointers on Playwriting.* Boston: The Writer, Inc., 1967.

Packard, William. *The Art of the Playwright*. New York: Paragon House Publishers, 1987.

Pike, Frank and Thomas G. Dunn. *The Playwright's Handbook*. New York: New American Library, 1985.

Smiley, Sam. *Playwriting: The Structure of Action*. Englewood Cliffs, New Jersey: Prentice-Hall, Inc., 1971.

Straczynski, J. Michael. *The Complete Book of Scriptwriting*. Cincinnati, Ohio: Writer's Digest Books, 1982.

Sweet, Jeffrey. *The Dramatist's Toolkit: The Craft of the Working Playwright*. Portsmouth, New Hampshire: Heinemann, 1993.

Williams, Tennessee. *Where I Live: Selected Essays*. New York: New Directions, 1978.

ABOUT THE AUTHOR

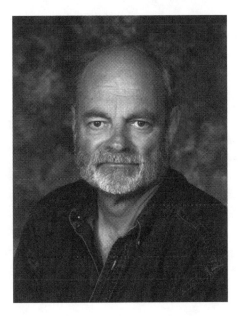

Marsh Cassady has written more than forty books including novels, short story and drama collections, haiku, biography, and books on theatre and storytelling. His audio and stage plays have been widely performed (including off-Broadway), and he has written and recorded a three-set audio tape on storytelling.

A former actor/director and university professor with a Ph.D. degree in theatre, Cassady has worked with more than a hundred productions. Currently fiction/drama editor of *Crazyquilt Quarterly*, he also co-edits a commercial magazine. Since 1981, he has conducted an all-genre writing workshop in San Diego and has taught various creative writing classes at UCSD and elsewhere. While teaching at Montclair State in the 1970s, he started a program of workshops, classes and special projects in playwriting. His own writing has won numerous regional and national awards.

ORDER FORM

MERIWETHER PUBLISHING LTD.
P.O. BOX 7710
COLORADO SPRINGS, CO 80933
TELEPHONE: (719) 594-4422

Please send me the following books:

_____ **Characters in Action #TT-B106** $14.95
by Marsh Cassady
Playwriting the easy way

_____ **The Theatre and You #TT-B115** $14.95
by Marsh Cassady
An introductory text on all aspects of theatre

_____ **Acting Games — Improvisations and** $12.95
Exercises #TT-B168
by Marsh Cassady
A textbook of theatre games and improvisations

_____ **The Art of Storytelling #TT-B139** $12.95
by Marsh Cassady
Creative ideas for preparation and performance

_____ **Theatre Games for Young** $12.95
Performers #TT-B188
by Maria C. Novelly
Improvisations and exercises for developing acting skills

_____ **Truth in Comedy #TT-B164** $12.95
by Charna Halpern, Del Close and Kim "Howard" Johnson
The manual of improvisation

_____ **The Scenebook for Actors #TT-B177** $14.95
by Norman A. Bert, Ph.D.
Great monologs and dialogs for auditions

**These and other fine Meriwether Publishing books are available at
your local bookstore or direct from the publisher. Use the handy order
form on this page.**

NAME: _____

ORGANIZATION NAME: _____

ADDRESS: _____

CITY:_____ STATE: _____ ZIP: _____

PHONE: _____

❑ **Check Enclosed**
❑ **Visa or MasterCard #** _____

Expiration
Signature: _____ *Date:* _____
(required for Visa/Mastercard orders)

COLORADO RESIDENTS: Please add 3% sales tax.
SHIPPING: Include $2.75 for the first book and 50¢ for each additional book ordered.

❑ *Please send me a copy of your complete catalog of books and plays.*